ELIZABETHAN PLYMOUTH
A PICTORIAL REVIEW

Chris Robinson

With a foreword by

HRH The Duke of Edinburgh KG

Lord High Steward of Plymouth

British Library Cataloguing in Publication Data
Robinson Chris 1954 -
Elizabethan Plymouth, A Pictorial Review 1952-2002
1.Devon. Plymouth, history
1. Title
942.3'58

ISBN 0 9510747 8 4 (7 6 for paperback)

Designed by Chris Robinson
Pictures scanned by Chris and Ben Robinson

First published October 2002

OTHER CHRIS ROBINSON TITLES
PUBLISHED BY PEN & INK

PLYMOUTH AS TIME DRAWS ON - 1985

PLYMOUTH AS TIME DRAWS ON VOL :2 - 1988

VICTORIAN PLYMOUTH: AS TIME DRAWS ON - 1991

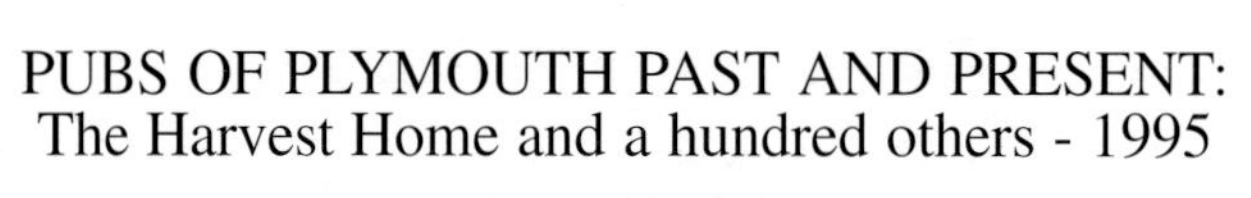

PUBS OF PLYMOUTH PAST AND PRESENT:
The Harvest Home and a hundred others - 1995

PUBS OF PLYMOUTH PAST AND PRESENT:
Prince George and a hundred others - 1997

UNION STREET - 2000

THE ARGYLE BOOK - 2002

Published by
Pen & Ink Publishing
34 New Street,
Barbican
Plymouth PL1 2NA
Tel 01752 705337/228120
Fax 01752 770001
www.chrisrobinson.co.uk

Printed & bound in Great Britain by
Latimer Trend & Company Ltd
Estover Close
Plymouth PL6 7PL
Devon

ELIZABETHAN PLYMOUTH
A PICTORIAL REVIEW
—Chris Robinson—

FOREWORD

By His Royal Highness
The Duke of Edinburgh

Having spent thirteen years with the Royal Navy, I should have spent part of that time based at Devonport and had a chance to visit Plymouth. As it happens I was always elsewhere, but I visited Plymouth not long after the war and I have vivid recollections of the dreadful state the City was in after the blitz.

I was then invited to become Lord High Steward and this appointment kept me in close touch with the mammoth task of re-building the City. Each time I have visited Plymouth in recent years, there has not been just the re-building to admire, but a whole series of new developments.

All this has taken place during the last fifty years and I am sure that the citizens of Plymouth, and many more beyond, will welcome this record of a very important period in the life of one of England's great historic cities.

Philip

INTRODUCTION

The rationale for this project was sparked by the idea of producing something to mark the Queen's Jubilee - a fifty-year period that has entirely encompassed my life and has witnessed the virtual rebirth of Plymouth and its total eclipse of the two other partners in former triumvirate that was known as the Three Towns. At the beginning of the Victorian era, Devonport was the largest of the Three Towns and Stonehouse was approaching its population peak. Logically it was inevitable that Plymouth would one day become the dominant partner; Stonehouse had no room to expand and Devonport was a virtual fortress, which by the middle of the nineteenth century had little undeveloped space left. However it was the destruction suffered during the Second World War which really gave the planners the chance to promote Plymouth at the expense of the other two, and consequently the only major shops and stores to be built in the immediate post-war years were erected on the 72 acres of prime development land cleared in the heart of city centre. Later, shops, services and superstores were created for the new housing estates and on the edge-of-town industrial estates, but not in Stonehouse or Devonport. This book is an attempt to chronicle that period in words and particularly in pictures. Doubtless there are omissions - events not mentioned, personalities not featured - but it is a fairly comprehensive account, and whatever its shortcomings it is certainly the most thorough review of the period in existence! No-one writing from this perspective can tell us how later historians will come to look back on this second great Elizabethan age, but the one thing we can be sure of is we know it because we've lived through it. As Max Boyce would say: "I was there!" Does that make our own view too specific, so that we can't see the wood for the trees? I don't think so. We live in a society that has never been better informed, not only about itself, but about other societies, other countries... other worlds. And as far as Plymouth itself is concerned, over the last few decades I've drawn it from hundreds of angles and written about it, photographed it and helped make films about it, so hopefully this is a reasonably well-informed and only slightly subjective account that will appeal not just to Plymothians past and present but also those of the future.

This is PLYMOUTH
THIS IS PLYMOUTH
PLYMOUTH 2000

Saturday, July 21, 2001
Your Weekend
A Way day special

THE VOICE OF PLYMOUTH
EVENING Herald
LOW PRICE TRAVEL INSURANCE
ANNUAL MULTITRIP WORLDWIDE COVER
Telephone 01752 364186
Tuesday, June 25, 2002
City & Districts
30p

LOOKING BACK
TAKE A TRIP DOWN MEMORY LANE WITH CHRIS ROBINSON – SEE PAGES 14 & 15

UNION STREET
CHRIS ROBINSON

VICTORIAN ILLUSTRATED As Time Draws On PLYMOUTH
Chris Robinson

PLYMOUTH
As Time Draws On

PLYMOUTH
As Time Draws On: Vol. 2

O·B
HARVEST HOME
and a hundred others
PLYMOUTH PUBS PAST & PRESENT
Chris Robinson

OLD PLYMOUTH
Today

A Video-Ex Production
Presented by
Chris Robinson

PLYMOUTH
Before the War
A Video-Ex Production
Presented by
Chris Robinson

PLYMOUTH
The War Years
An Alan Tibbitts Video-Ex Production
Presented by
Chris Robinson

This is
PLYMOUTH

PLYMOUTH
2000
An Alan Tibbitts Production
Presented by
Chris Robinson

CO-OP STORE (FIRST PART) ROYAL PARADE—

Shopping Centre of Reconstructed Plymouth

A store of beauty and utility, commanding the interest of the discerning shopper and pride of over 93,000 Co-operative members

. . . . .

Expressive of adventurous enterprise in public service, and coincident in opening with a new era

Completed in Coronation Year (1953) Elizabeth II

The Co-op was one of the first big stores to appear in the new Plymouth City Centre. Phase one was completed in the Coronation Year. The Plymouth Co-operative Society had, as it happily proclaimed at the time, maintained service to households of its members during six reigns. Established in 1860, during the reign of Queen Victoria, it originally had 90 members and annual sales of £498. At the beginning of Queen Elizabeth's reign that figure had increased to 93,000 members with annual sales of £5.2 million. Fifty years later the membership had increased to 138,000 and the annual trunover to £126 million. The Co-op remains the largest independent and only locally-controlled department store in the City Centre. Renamed Derrys in 1998, the main store continues to evolve, while as an organisation Plymouth & South West Co-operative (as it is called now) has responsibility for 85 other local retail outlets. In 2000 the Co-op celebrated its 140th birthday with the marking-out and promoting of a 15-mile inner-city walk, The Co-operative Way, taking in and helping to maintain several nature reserves, as the organisation remains committed to the City and its citizens.

Co-operative
Greengrocery Service.
CO-OP
361
GDR 997

SALE
Souvenirs
of
PLYMOUTH
&

SALE
SALE
TIGHTS AND

CO-OPERATIVE HOUSE

COME
CO·OPERATIVE
SHOPPING
For all the family
Plymouth & South Devon Co-operative Society Ltd.

THE
GOOD THINGS
IN LIFE
COME FROM
PLYMOUTH
CO-OPERATIV

OOTWEAR
THE
SPICE OF LIFE
COMES FROM
PLYMOUTH
CO-OPERATIVE
FASHIONS
FOOD
MENSWEAR
URNISHINGS

the
Difference
is Derrys
GINA BACCONI
For the latest in stylish Evening Wear and special occasion dressing.
REGATTA
Main stockists of the new ranges from this top Casual Wear brand.

ELIZABETHAN PLYMOUTH

Queen Elizabeth I reigned for almost 45 years, the longest of any of the Tudor monarchs. However, in all that time Elizabeth never once visited the town, a town without whose support and sailors her reign may well have been very much shorter. But Plymouth not only provided Her Majesty with great seamen and safe harbouring of her ships, it also benefitted greatly from the spoils of war - and of piracy. The late 16th century was a boom time for the town, then the principal port of Devon. Plymouth Dock (or Devonport as it became) was still a century away. The Barbican, very much part of old Plymouth today, largely came into being during the time of Elizabeth I, the local population increased, and Plymouth's first speculative property developers became active. The whole Elizabethan period was a busy and prosperous time for the town and yet the Queen would have had very little idea of what it was like - the odd topographical drawing or map, perhaps, maybe even a painting - but generally there was very little in the way of a visual record for the Virgin Queen, the last of her line and the last British monarch to have died unmarried. Queen Elizabeth II has reigned for 50 years, the longest of any of the members of the House of Windsor, and longer than any other monarch - apart from Queen Victoria and George III - in the last 500 years. During that fifty-year period the Queen has visited the City on a number of occasions, as indeed has her husband, the Duke of Edinburgh (the Lord High Steward of Plymouth since 1960) and Prince Charles, Prince Andrew and Princess Anne. Like the first, this second great Elizabethan age has also been marked by a period of great expansion for Plymouth, although had the Blitz not precipitated redevelopment and the subsequent redrawing of the city limits (leading to a doubling of acreage), it is interesting to speculate on how much more slowly change might have occurred. But the changes have occurred - and how great they have been, such that whatever else history may have to say about this Elizabethan age it is sure to rate it among the most significant in the City's rich and varied heritage. And from the Queen Mother laying the foundation stone to Royal Parade with her husband George VI in 1947, through the young Princess Elizabeth laying a stone to commemorate the rebuilding of the City's mother church, St Andrew's, in 1949, her opening of the Civic Centre as Queen in 1962, her unveiling of the Sundial in 1988, and any number of other significant local events, in the Dockyard, Royal William Yard and Manadon, there can be no doubting that this Elizabeth knows the City well, because she, too, can say: "I was there!"

6 5 4 3 2 1 12
5
4
3
2

1950

Hector Stirling won approval for a plan to rebuild the Guildhall in a way that satisfied the sentimentalists and avoided the defects of the old hall. Plans followed for a Concert Hall to the south of the Guildhall. Tamerton Foliot and part of Bickleigh come within the new Plymouth boundary and the final decision was taken on the Dockyard Extension; 50 acres would be appropriated by the Admiralty, not the 220 they had been looking at in 1945. The workforce in the yard incidentally had dropped to 15,338 - it had been 17,793 just after the war. There was also a reduction in Plymouth's parliamentary representation - from three seats to two and in the February election Michael Foot held Devonport while fellow Labour candidate Lucy Middleton held Sutton. Argyle meanwhile won very little; just three wins after Christmas 1949; they failed to score in 10 of their last 15 matches. There was one moment of joy as they drew 1-1 with Cup holders Wolverhampton Wanderers in the third round at home in front of 40,000, thanks to a goal from the £6,000 signing from Aberdeen, Stan Williams. Sadly they failed to score in the replay and lost 3-0. The City had its first post-war Carnival, Prime Minister Atlee visited Royal Parade, Woolworth's - the first big store of the new City Centre - reopened, as work began on the Norwich Union Building, Marks & Spencer's and Pennycomequick roundabout.

Who is Britain's "SPORTSMAN OF THE YEAR"?
Make sure YOUR vote is included in the Annual National Ballot organised by
SPORTING RECORD
The Family All-Sports Paper — Every week 3d
Send your vote to: "VOTES," 184 FLEET STREET, E.C.4
GET YOUR FRIENDS TO VOTE AS WELL

JANUARY 7th, 1950 — Kick-off 2.15 p.m.

F.A. Challenge Cup, 3rd round

PLYMOUTH ARGYLE

WOLVERHAMPTON WANDERERS

Official Souvenir Programme 6d.

PALE A ALE
The Best Bitter in the West of England
THE PLYMOUTH BREWERIES LTD.

OUR NEXT MEETING
THURS., APRIL 27th at 7.45 p.m.
Southern League Match
VERSUS
Walthamstow
including
J. BOYD H. EDWARDS C. MAY
D. GEARY R. REEVES
THIS SEASONS THIRD OFFICIAL FIXTURE
ALSO
BILL KITCHEN
(WEMBLEY)
THURSDAY NIGHT IS SPEEDWAY NIGHT

Greyhound Racing
HURDLES and FLAT
AT THIS STADIUM
EVERY WED. and SAT.

1951

The distinctive old Prudential building is demolished, Timothy Whites, Dolcis, Woodhouse & Sons, and Willson's are new arrivals in New George Street, and on 1 September Dingles, the first new complete departmental store to be rebuilt in the country, complete with the area's first escalator, opens two-and-a-half floors and an eager crowd of 40,000 filter through the doors. Sir John Burnet is the Architect. In October the foundation stone of the new Pearl Assurance Building is laid and the following month Marks & Spencer's starts trading again in Old Town Street. Actress Mercy Haystead follows Ann Crawford in opening another new store, this time it's Harwood's Shoe Store in the Norwich Union Building. The Register Office moves from 13 Thorn Park to 7 Belle Vue Place, North Hill; Alexandra Road, Mutley, is widened at the top end and the field behind the Greyhound Stadium becomes the first big private housing estate since the war. Lancaster Gardens, Whitleigh, is occupied for the first time and Whitleigh Footbridge opens. With a span of 362ft it's the longest of its kind in the country. New Gas Board offices are authorised, Prince Rock Power Station comes to life, and Dartmoor is designated a National Park. Beer is just over a shilling (5p) a pint and the newly-relegated Argyle are again dumped out of the FA Cup by Wolves, this time at home in front of a 40,000 crowd.

CORONA

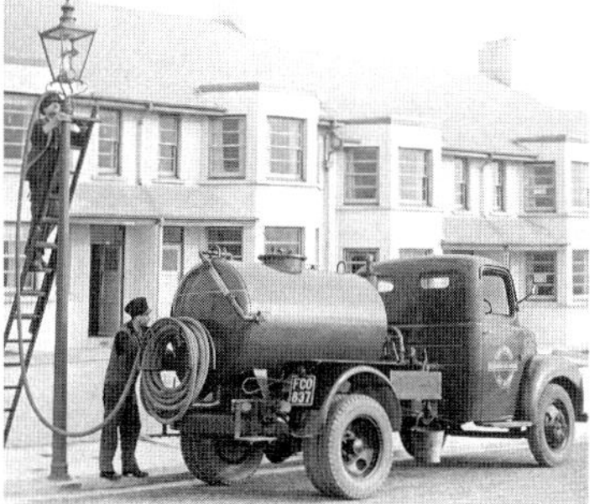

NAAFI
CLUB
CAFETERIA
INNER LOUNGE
TAVERN
PLYMOUTH

YE BLACK BOY

1952

The second great Elizabethan era was ushered in on 6 February 1952 when news broke that King George VI had died in the early hours of the morning. A heavy smoker, the King, who had lung cancer, suffered a heart attack. He was just 56 years old. Princess Elizabeth, holidaying in Kenya, made plans to return immediately. In Plymouth, too, a new era was dawning; Tin Pan Alley, the Corn Exchange and old Meat Market all closed as work began on the new Pannier Market. Work on removing the forlorn iron framework of the blitzed Pier was started, and a beginning was made on extending the War Memorial. New buildings included Montague Burtons, Old Town Street, Barclays Bank, Princess Square and the first phase of the new Co-operative. Princess Margaret opened the new Naafi club in Notte Street with Lord Mayor Henry Wright while other new developments included Drake Primary School in Keyham, the conversion of Budshead Barn into Ernesettle Library, and a roundabout at the southern end of Mutley Plain. Waldorf Astor, Plymouth's wartime mayor, died, Colin Campbell was knighted, and the telephone exchanges at St Budeaux and Devonport were automated. Argyle's attack spearheaded by Astall, Rattray, Govan, Dews and Tadman, propelled them to the top of Division Three South. Shortt, Radcliffe, Jones and Chisholm played in every game of the campaign.

TOMORROW
(Thursday), December 4th, at 9 a.m.
WE OPEN THE FIRST FLOOR OF
OUR NEW STORE

ROYAL PARADE, PLYMOUTH

BEAUTIFULLY CARPETED AND APPOINTED SHOWROOMS FOR FASHIONS

COATS - GOWNS - FURS - KNITWEAR - BLOUSES
UNDERWEAR - CORSETS - BRASSIERES - JUVENILE
- BABY LINEN - CARPETS & LINOLEUM

10,000 Sq. Yds. FELT BASE FLOOR COVERING
S.C.W.S. Make (Selected Lengths). Attractive Patterns.
OFFERED AT 2/- Sq. Yd.

See Our Window Displays

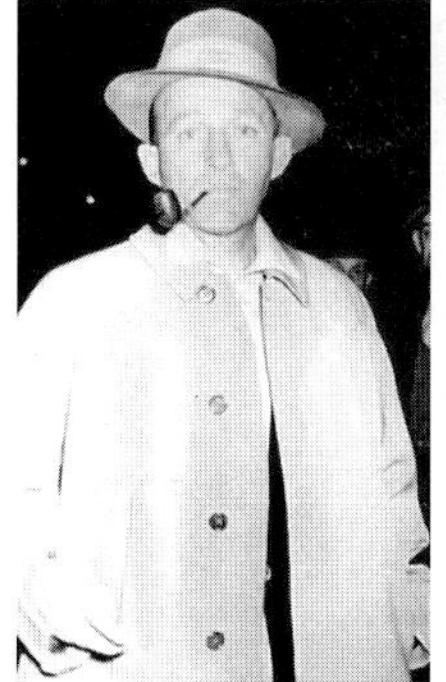

UNDER ENTIRELY NEW MANAGEMENT
CHECKERS CAFE
RUSSELL STREET
(4 doors from Vospers Radio)
will give you a hearty welcome BEFORE & AFTER THE MATCH
A VARIETY OF GOOD FOOD AT A PRICE TO SUIT YOUR POCKET
Parties up to 200 catered for — Telephone 2481

JAN. 12th. 1952
Kick-off 2.45 p.m.

FOOTBALL LEAGUE DIVISION III (SOUTH)

Plymouth Argyle

Exeter City

OFFICIAL PROGRAMME 3d

COMPLETE NAVAL AND CIVILIAN
TAILORS AND OUTFITTERS
A. FLEMING & CO. (Outfitters) LTD.
CONTRACTORS TO THE ADMIRALTY
9 JOHNSTON TERRACE — KEYHAM
BRANCHES IN ALL PRINCIPAL PORTS — Telephone 113

NEVER MISS YOUR LITTLEWOODS
-IT MAY BE YOUR TURN NEXT!
LITTLEWOODS
The world's largest and best Football Pool
LITTLEWOODS POOLS LTD. LIVERPOOL

HILL LANE
Junior Lawn Tennis Club
Hartley, Plymouth

Spring Tournament
Programme

Programme — *Price 4d.*

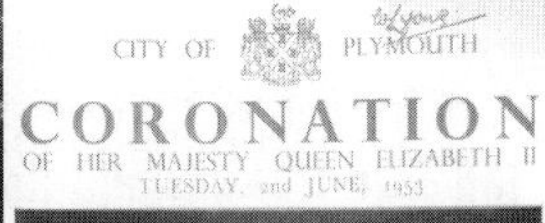

1953

Plymouth Hoe, with the Royal Citadel, was the setting for the historical Pageant of Plymouth Hoe. Crispin Gill wrote and Cyril Penrose produced the episodic spectacular which was staged between 18 and 25 July. The last vestiges of the Pier had been cleared, new buildings included John Yeo's, Boots, Timothy Whites, Popplestones and Pilgrim Congregational Church at Milehouse. There was new Corporation housing on the site of Stoke House, the Cecil Street, star-type flats were opened, and John Laing & Son built Plymouth's 2,000th Easiform house, in Ross Street, Devonport. New shops appeared in Whitleigh, there were new changing facilities for footballers in Central Park and floodlights were used at Home Park for the first time "on a miserable night" for a friendly against Exeter City. Plymouth's first flashing beacons were erected to aid pedestrians in Royal Parade and a new bus station was created in the east end of Union Street, just across from the newly completed GEC building. The old Sugar Refinery was demolished, Sir Colin Campbell retired and was succeeded by Stuart Lloyd Jones who arrived to find that local unemployment figures were twice that of the national average. HMS *Salisbury*, the first ship to be built in Devonport Dockyard since the war, was launched in June and the newly-promoted Argyle finished a creditable fourth in Division Two.

1953
CORONATION
SEALS
PRICE SIXPENCE

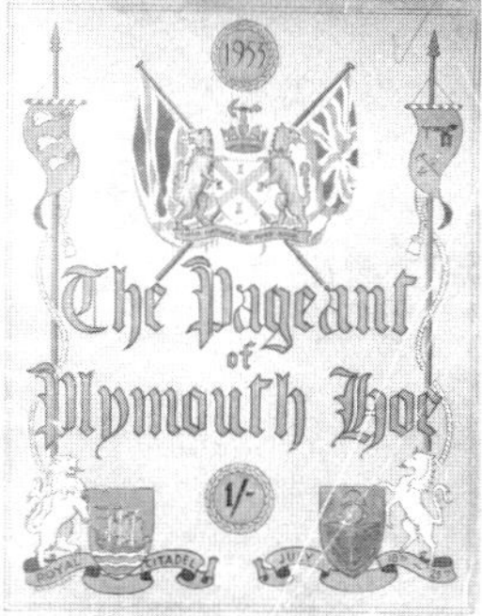

Plymouth Argyle
versus
Gateshead

OFFICIAL PROGRAMME 3d.

COMPLETE NAVAL AND CIVILIAN
TAILORS AND OUTFITTERS
A. FLEMING & Co. (Outfitters) Ltd.
Contractors to the Admiralty
9, JOHNSTON TERRACE KEYHAM
Branches in all Principal Ports

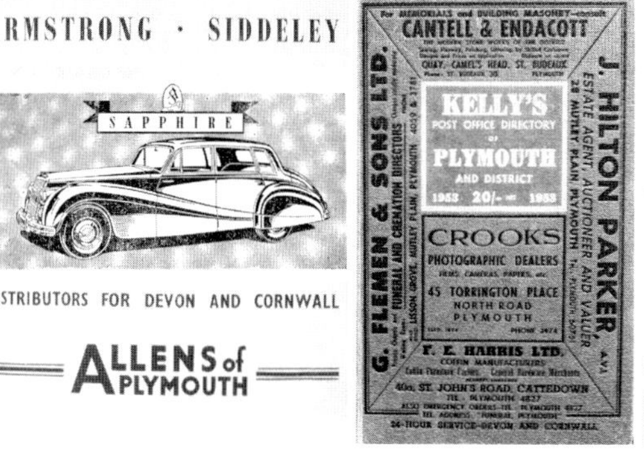

Radiant House, the new Gas HQ, is completed and the second phase of the Co-operative gets under way. In New George Street the new Electricity Service Centre opens, so too do both Costers and Hornes. The actress Sandra Dorne cuts the ribbon at the Modella Fashion House and Winnicott Brothers start operating from their new offices and warehouse in Ebrington Street. More star-type flats are built, at West Hoe, opposite the old rinkeries, in Notte Street, on the Barbican and at Boons Place. New housing estates at Penlee and Pennycross start to take shape, Plymouth's first self-help homes are completed in Elgin Crescent, and in Devonport work on the Dockyard extension is well under way. A new branch of the Union Savings Bank is also opened there as are a number of new Army flats. The impressive Tudor mansion, Widey Court, is demolished to make way for a new primary school, Pennycross Junior Mixed is occupied for the first time and Princess Margaret is back in Plymouth to unveil the extension to the War Memorial on the Hoe. The Princess also unveils a tablet commemorating the rebuilding of the Central Library. The Octagon Brewery is taken over by H&G Simmonds of Reading, while Argyle fall back to 19th in the second division - among the season's highlights, a 4-0 victory over Everton at Home Park followed by an 8-4 defeat in the return match in February at Goodison.

PALACE THEATRE Plymouth

Man. Dir.: Gerard Heath Gen. Man.: William Willis
Telephone 4383 and 5347/8

NEXT WEEK COMMENCING MAY 17th, 1954
6.20 TWICE NIGHTLY 8.35
MATINEE ON SATURDAY AT 2.30

BERNARD DELFONT presents . . .
The PERSONAL VISIT of
Hollywood's Greatest Comedy Couple
STAN OLIVER
LAUREL & HARDY

In a New Comedy: "Birds of a Feather"
with a Gigantic Family Variety Programme, including
★ THE WONDER HORSE "TONY"
★ HARRY WORTH ★ TRIO BOTANDO
★ KAYE'S PEKINESE PETS
★ ALAN ROWE ★ LORRAINE
★ MARY & MICHAEL MILLS
★ DOROTHY REID & MACK

Make up your party and Book NOW!

4/6, 4/-, 3/6, 2/6 and 1/6
FREE LIST ENTIRELY SUSPENDED

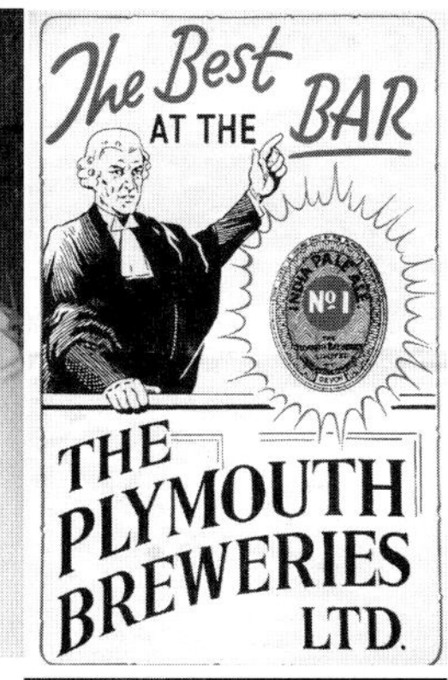

FLOODLIGHTING of HOME PARK

MADGE & SON

Home Park : Plymouth

Football League Division 2. Kick-off 3.0 p.m.

Saturday, October 24th, 1953

Plymouth Argyle
versus
Notts County

OFFICIAL PROGRAMME 3d.

COMPLETE NAVAL AND CIVILIAN TAILORS AND OUTFITTERS
A. FLEMING & Co. (Outfitters) Ltd.
Contractors to the Admiralty
9, JOHNSTON TERRACE :: KEYHAM
(opposite R.N.E. Main Gate)
Branches in all Principal Ports at Home and Overseas
Telephone 113

Published by Plymouth Argyle Football Co. Ltd.

1955

One of the big surprises in the Election this year was the defeat of Michael Foot in the Devonport Constituency; local ward reorganisation and perhaps more importantly a national swing to the Conservatives were largely responsible for Joan Vickers' success there. Jacob Astor held on to the Sutton seat he had first won in 1951. Among the many new buildings to go up around the city were two churches at Glenholt and Ernesettle. St John, Sutton-on-Plym meanwhile celebrated its centenary in the same year that its longest serving incumbent, Francis Sanderson, died in office. New schools included Burleigh and Penlee (the former Stuart Road Secondary) and there was new housing at Manadon. Freedom Fields hospital was fitted out with a new casualty department, while in town it was estimated that some 80% of Royal Parade and New George Street had been completed. The Carmenians' big show of the year was the *Lilac Domino,* while the Tamaritans staged *The River Line*, *Thark*, *The Happy Journey*, *Affairs Of The State* and *Dial M For Murder*. The number of passenger ships calling here hit a peak of 187, with some 29,000 passengers passing through the port, while Argyle, now without the services of the mighty Jumbo Chisholm, forced into early retirement by various injuries, and perhaps even his fondness for drink, dropped a further place down the second division order.

Home Park : Plymouth

F.A. CHALLENGE CUP — Third Round

Saturday, January 8th, 1955

Plymouth Argyle

Newcastle United

Kick off 2.15 p.m.

OFFICIAL PROGRAMME 3d.

COMPLETE NAVAL AND CIVILIAN TAILORS AND OUTFITTERS

A. FLEMING & Co. (Outfitters) Ltd.

Contractors to the Admiralty

9, JOHNSTON TERRACE :: KEYHAM

(opposite R.N.B. Main Gate)

Branches in all Principal Ports at Home and Overseas

Telephone 113

The Queen Mother was driven along the flight deck of HMS *Ark Royal* when she came to visit Devonport Dockyard, Princess Alexandra laid the foundation stone for the Church of the Ascension at Crownhill, and writer, artist, broadcaster and ornithologist Peter Scott was here to open the reconstructed Central Library. St Peter's Church was also rebuilt and reconsecrated, and work began on the rebuilding of North Road Station. The former gunnery range at Wembury became HMS *Cambridge*, the first 300 houses on the Southway Estate were completed and the last buses with wooden seats were withdrawn from service. The year also saw the issue of the last white £5 notes. You could buy a new winter coat with one of these notes and still have plenty of change; to put it in another context, a new semi-detached house on the Davis estate in Plympton would cost something in the order of £2,125. Television had started to gain an audience here, broadcasting began each day at five for children, then stopped for an hour - the toddler's truce - picking up again at 7pm and running through to 11pm. The cinemas - Odeon, Royal, Gaumont, Plaza, Forum, State, Ford Palladium and the Belgrave, Mutley - were all doing good business, but struggling Argyle weren't. 21,236 watched their first home match that season but only 6,661 their last as they were relegated from the Second Division.

CAFE
SIMONDS BEER

COMPTON SERVICE STATION

The higher one climbs
in the Service
the more one appreciates
PLYMOUTH GIN

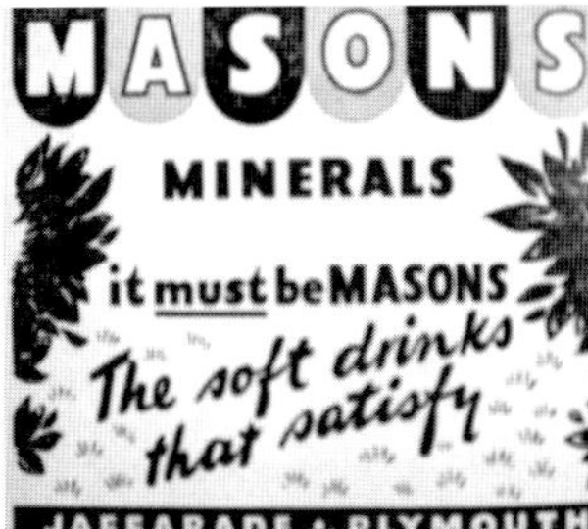
MASONS
MINERALS
it must be MASONS
The soft drinks that satisfy
JAFFARADE • PLYMOUTH

BON APPETIT
PEDRO'S OCTAGON RESTAURANT ! ! !
PEDRO'S OCTAGON RESTAURANT
(FULLY LICENSED)
The Octagon, Plymouth
Tel. 60417

PLYMOUTH
DELIGHTFUL CENTRE FOR HOLIDAYS

PALACE THEATRE
PLYMOUTH

PLYMOUTH ARGYLE
Versus
BRISTOL ROVERS
Home Park - Plymouth
Monday
April 2nd
1956
FOOTBALL LEAGUE DIVISION II
KICK OFF 3.15 p.m.
OFFICIAL PROGRAMME - 3d.
FLOODLIGHTING of HOME PARK
MADGE & SON

BEECHWOOD
Where do all the Good Pigs go?
....INTO BEECHWOOD SAUSAGES & HOGS PUDDINGS OF COURSE!

1957

The Mayflower replica attracted large crowds when it appeared in the Sound, there were a few curious onlookers too who made it down to the Barbican to see HMS *Amethyst*, the Yangtse hero, being broken up on Marrowbone Slip. The Mayflower pub, at Ernesettle, became the first new licensed premises on a post-war estate, meanwhile the Old Ring Of Bells in Woolster Street was the latest Tudor casualty of Plymouth's post-war planning. The Wellington in Union Street was also demolished. The rebuilding of St Andrew's Church was completed - it was rededicated on St Andrew's Day. St Chad's was also rededicated - to St Lo - and became the Dockyard Church. With more car drivers on the roads than ever, the Oreston and Turnchapel Steamboat Co decided to stop their service to Turnchapel. Night flying was now allowed at Roborough, not far north of the new Slumberland Mattress factory. Browne & Sharpe machine tools were another new firm in town and set up a base in Ernesettle, while over at Whitleigh, Clark's claimed that they would be producing 12,000 pairs of shoes per week from their Plymouth factory within 14 months. It was also estimated that since 1950 some 2,200 new dwellings had gone up in Whitleigh, housing a population of around 10,000. Remarkably, between 1951 and 1957 over 1,000 permanent council houses were built in the city each year.

BY
BLIGHT & WHITE LTD.

1958

The Duke of Edinburgh came to Plymouth and visited the City Centre, the Barbican and the new 102-bedroomed YMCA building at the top of Armada Way. Pophams, the last of the major department stores to be rebuilt in the City Centre, opened; so too did the award-winning National Westminster Bank - built by Humphreys - at the end of Royal Parade. Pymouth's first post-war cinema, the Drake - the first of a projected chain from 20th Century Fox - debuted on 6 June with a charity premiere of South Pacific. A few months earlier the bus station moved from its temporary Union Street home to purpose-built premises at Breton Side. Friary Railway Station became a goods yard and North Road Station was renamed Plymouth Station. Southway Junior School admitted its first pupils, the Royal Marine pub in Efford opened and Methodist Central Hall continued to be used for Mayor Choosing and other Civic occasions. The Church of the Ascension at Crownhill was dedicated while St Catherine's Church at the bottom of Lockyer Street was demolished. Argyle were all but annihilated as Newcastle put six past goalkeeper Geoff Barnsley at Home Park, in the third round of the FA Cup. Wilf Carter provided the only scrap of joy for the Pilgrims in front of a 38,000-strong crowd. The Greens' league form improved though - they finished third in the last season of the old Division Three South.

YMCA

ALLENS of PLYMOUTH
105 TAVISTOCK ROAD
Bring the family to see the
Vauxhall Victor

The Keppel's Head
KEPPELS HEAD

THE CITY'S OWN ANNUAL
PLYMOUTH CHEER

Costers LTD
NEW GEORGE ST PLYMOUTH
LADIES' KNITWEAR
TWIN SETS
CARDIGANS and
GOR-RAY
SKIRTS
Jacoll
HATS
UNDERWEAR

Plymouth Argyle Football Club.
3D
RESURGAM
3D
OFFICIAL PROGRAMME
PLYMOUTH ARGYLE v. SUNDERLAND
KICK-OFF
SEASON
1957-58
SAFELY ENTRUST ALL YOUR ELECTRICAL REQUIREMENTS TO
PORTLAND SQUARE
MADGE & SON
PLYMOUTH
TEL 63315

SOUVENIR PROGRAMME
1958
R.A.F.A.
Battle of Britain Week
ROYAL AIR FORCES ASSOCIATION
Patron:
H. M. THE QUEEN
Incorporated by Royal Charter
PLYMOUTH BRANCH
Registered under the War Charities Act, 1940
PLEASE GIVE GENEROUSLY
SEPTEMBER 15th 21th
PRICE: 6d

BBC
symphony concerts
THEATRE ROYAL

On Saturday 5 September and on the following Monday the new Pannier Market opened. Designed by Walls & Pearn, the new building cost £269,548. Later that same month Widey Technical School became the most modern educational establishment in Plymouth and then on 24 September Field Marshal Montgomery opened the reconstructed Plymouth Guildhall. Outside work began on the demolition of the remaining buildings of pre-war Westwell Street to make way for the proposed Civic Centre. Work also began on the new Laira Bridge and the Farley Factory in Hartley was enlarged. Meanwhile in a small shed in Newport Street, Stonehouse, the firm Marine Projects was born. The Heybrook Bay Motor Services Company which operated buses to Heybrook Bay and Bovisand was sold to Western National. The Palace Theatre, experiencing difficult times, became a Bingo Hall and Night Club, Plympton Station was closed, and St John the Baptist Church at Devonport was demolished. The new Aggie Westons building opened and St James The Less at Ham was consecrated. The Royal Dockyard College moved into the vacated Keyham College buildings and James Paton-Watson, the City Engineer and joint architect of the visionary 1943 Plan For Plymouth, retired. Wilf Carter and Jimmy Gauld spearheaded Argyle's Championship success in the newly-created 3rd Division.

LONDON

ESSO
GREETINGS
FROM
GLENHOLT CARAVAN PARK

BATTLE OF BRITAIN
WEEK
1959
R.A.F.A.
ROYAL AIR FORCES ASSOCIATION
H.M. THE QUEEN
PLYMOUTH BRANCH
Souvenir Programme
PLEASE GIVE GENEROUSLY

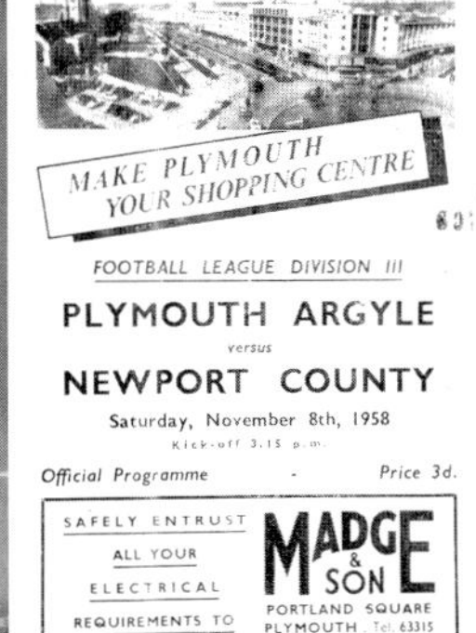

MAKE PLYMOUTH
YOUR SHOPPING CENTRE
FOOTBALL LEAGUE DIVISION III
PLYMOUTH ARGYLE
versus
NEWPORT COUNTY
Saturday, November 8th, 1958
Kick-off 3.15 p.m.
Official Programme - Price 3d.
SAFELY ENTRUST
ALL YOUR
ELECTRICAL
REQUIREMENTS TO
MADGE & SON
PORTLAND SQUARE
PLYMOUTH Tel. 63315

THE NAVAL APPROACH

The DRAKE
PLYMOUTH
SUNDAY, 20th SEPTEMBER
at 3 p.m.
ON THE STAGE . . .
MAX JAFFA TRIO
FIRST VISIT TO PLYMOUTH
PLYMOUTH LADIES' CHOIR
DOROTHY HARWOOD
WYN CALVIN
The Royal Air Forces Association
PLYMOUTH BRANCH
present
Commemoration
Sunday
ON THE SCREEN . . .
A TRIBUTE TO
"THE FEW" AND BRITAIN
The
"Battle
of Britain"
FIRST SCREENING IN PLYMOUTH
ALL SEATS
BOOKABLE IN
ADVANCE . . .
Stalls 5/-
Circle 10/6; 7/6; 5/-
BOX OFFICE NOW OPEN

PLYMOUTH SPORTS' STADIUM
PENNYCROSS, PLYMOUTH
GOOD FRIDAY, 27th MARCH, 1959
AT 3.15 P.M.
DEVILS v. MIDLANDS
and West of England Match Race
Official Souvenir Programme 1/-.

1960

The shape of the city centre continued to change and the traces of pre-war Plymouth were getting fewer and farther between. Popular culture was also changing. Television sets were cheaper to buy or rent (6d in the slot), skiffle and rock and roll paved the way for beat groups, and yet still the dance bands pulled big crowds - Frankie Fuge, George Day, Ted Coleman, Les Colmer, Les Watts, Harry Brown - with the Guildhall, the Duke of Cornwall and the Prince Regent among the most popular venues. Rod Mason's New Jazz Club added an extra dimension to the local music scene when it opened at the Embassy, Milehouse. In Devonport, Woolworth's opened a new store in Marlborough Street, but William Street was closed off prior to it becoming part of the expanding dockyard. Prince Rock Power Station reached full capacity - 220,000 kw - and the city went to the polls over the development of an airport at Harrowbeer. The Co-operative movement celebrated its centenary in Plymouth, the Church of the Holy Spirit was dedicated at Southway and the farthing ceased to be legal tender. We also had the introduction of the first banknote to bear a portrait of the Queen, and, in the absence of a formal foundation stone, the Duke of Edinburgh, two years after work had begun, unveiled a tablet in the wall of the Council House to mark his installation as Lord High Steward of Plymouth.

CENTRAL RESTAURANT
BACHELOR

K R ENDACOTE

Pale Ale

FOOTBALL LEAGUE DIVISION II
Plymouth Argyle
FOOTBALL CLUB
Saturday, 13th February, 1960
PLYMOUTH ARGYLE
versus
LIVERPOOL
Kick-off 3.15 p.m.
Official Programme Price 3d.

SAFELY ENTRUST
ALL YOUR
ELECTRICAL
REQUIREMENTS TO
MADGE & SON
PORTLAND SQUARE
PLYMOUTH Tel. 63315

TAKE SOME HOME
THEY
GO DOWN
WELL
LEAR'S
DRAKES
CUSHIONS
PAST PRESENT
& FUTURE ENJOYMENT
MADE BY LEAR BROS. LTD. PLYMOUTH
Quality
THE SECRET

A CITY OF PLYMOUTH ENTERTAINMENT
HOE SUMMER THEATRE
PLYMOUTH
HEDLEY
CLAXTON PRESENTS
GAY TIME
A SPARKLING SUMMER SHOW

PLYMOUTH
SPEEDWAY
Official Programme
6d.
Thursday, 8th September
7.30 p.m.
WESTERN CUP COMPETITION
Plymouth v. Bristol
RIGHT OF ADMISSION RESERVED

CHRISTMAS CHEER

On 24 October, the Saltash ferry made its last crossing of the Tamar after centuries of service; meanwhile there were high winds and driving rain for those making the first trips across the new road bridge. The new road crossing of the Laira had been opened earlier in the year by Lord Chesham, the Parliamentary Secretary to the Minister of Transport. That same month - June - saw the last day of the regular steam train service between Plymouth and Saltash. In town, the Westward Television premises were opened, as was the Athenaeum - which, it was hoped, the TV Company would use for its productions. Lord Mayor Arthur Goldberg opened the new theatre; the neighbouring Drake Cinema meanwhile was sold to the Rank Organisation and the Forum, Devonport, ceased operating as a cinema - boxing, bingo, roller-skating and wrestling were now the order of the day. The impact of TV was spreading as Westward started bringing Robin Hood, Candid Camera and the Avengers into our homes and the BBC started their News From the South West, read by Tom Salmon. Burrington School opened with Bill Button as head, while Plymouth-born Angela Mortimer won the ladies' singles at Wimbledon. Argyle finished 11th in Division II and, in the first ever League Cup competition, they took the eventual winners, Aston Villa, to two replays in the 4th round before losing 5-3 at home.

PLYMOUTH TRANSPORT

COFFEE HOUSE

Christmas Cheer
PLYMOUTH'S OWN MAGAZINE
Christmas 1961
Price 1/3

FOOTBALL LEAGUE DIVISION II
Plymouth Argyle
FOOTBALL CLUB
Wednesday, 31st August, 1960
PLYMOUTH ARGYLE
versus
SHEFFIELD UNITED
Kick-off 7.30 p.m.
Official Programme Price 4d.

SAFELY ENTRUST
ALL YOUR
ELECTRICAL
REQUIREMENTS TO
MADGE & SON
PORTLAND SQUARE
PLYMOUTH Tel. 63315

DUDLEY COLES LIMITED
BUILDING & CIVIL ENGINEERING CONTRACTORS
PLYMOUTH

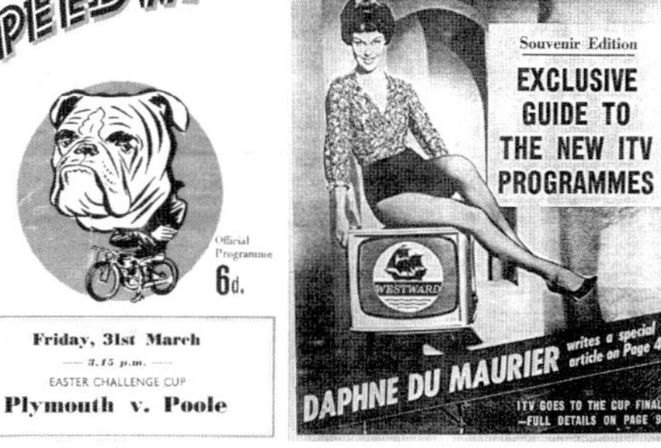
PLYMOUTH
SPEEDWAY
Official
Programme
6d.
Friday, 31st March
3.15 p.m.
EASTER CHALLENGE CUP
Plymouth v. Poole
SERVING DEVON CORNWALL SOMERSET DORSET
LOOK WESTWARD
Souvenir Edition
EXCLUSIVE
GUIDE TO
THE NEW ITV
PROGRAMMES
WESTWARD
DAPHNE DU MAURIER
writes a special article on Page 4
ITV GOES TO THE CUP FINAL
—FULL DETAILS ON PAGE 9

1962

In April the Queen Mother officially opened the Tamar Road Bridge;in July her daughter, Queen Elizabeth II, opened the new Civic Centre. The Council replaced the Hoe Summer Marquee with the single-storey Hoe Theatre. 29 Commando took up residence in the Citadel, the Register Office moved into the vacated Lord Mayor's Parlour in Portland Villas, Whitbread's took over Starkey Knight and Ford and Dingles took over the assets of Pophams. The Naval History Library moved from Mount Wise to the Central Library, the thrice-yearly entry of apprentices into the Dockyard increased the number on the Devonport Dockyard Technical College Register from 854 to 1,001, and Dewdney's pasties were either 8d or 1/4d. The Castle Inn at Mount Batten was demolished to make way for the Sergeants' Mess, the round tower at Mount Batten was saved from demolition thanks to the Old Plymouth Society and Stanley Goodman, while the former vicarage at St Budeaux, on the main road to the bridge, was converted as the Cornwall's Gate pub. The former Regent Cinema (Odeon from 1940) closed, and the old Gaumont in Union Street was renamed the Odeon; at the same time the old stalls of the Gaumont became the Majestic Ballroom - competition for the Park Ballroom. Southway School opened with head P Bindschedler and Dr Beeching opened the revamped Plymouth Station.

LIFTS
INFORMATION

NEWS
WORLD
INDIVIDUAL
DARTS
CHAMPIONSHIP

SOUTH AND WEST EDITION
JULY 21–27
BBC
Radio Times
tv and SOUND
5d
ROYAL
VISIT TO
PLYMOUTH
READ
Maigret
IN
RADIO TIMES

PLYMOUTH
SPEEDWAY
PENNYCROSS STADIUM, PLYMOUTH
MEETING No. 2
APRIL 12, 1962
PLYMOUTH v. SWINDON "B"

CITY OF PLYMOUTH
THE MUNICIPAL OFFICES
PRICE ONE SHILLING

FOOTBALL LEAGUE DIVISION II
Plymouth Argyle
FOOTBALL CLUB
Saturday, September 9th, 1961
PLYMOUTH ARGYLE
versus
MIDDLESBROUGH
Kick-off 3.15 p.m.
Official Programme Price 4d.
SAFELY ENTRUST
ALL YOUR
ELECTRICAL
REQUIREMENTS TO
MADGE & SON
PORTLAND SQUARE
PLYMOUTH Tel. 63315

Christmas Cheer
Plymouth's Own Magazine
1962
1/3

1963

The year opened with much of the South West snowbound, causing widespread chaos, as did the subsequent flooding in some areas. Commercially, the port was quieter than it had been, Plymouth's fishing fleet was down to just half a dozen trawlers, and the last Plymouth tender was laid up.The old Odeon Cinema was at last pulled down and Littlewoods' new store built on its site, and after various rescue plans had come to nothing, the old Grand Theatre in Union Street was also demolished. Clarks added another shoe factory to their Plymouth operation and there was a new roundabout created on Wolseley Road. Sir John Hunt was here in June to launch the new Ballard Centre, the loan sanction for the proposed new Central Park Swimming Pool was approved, and Lord Denning, Master of the Rolls, opened the City's new Law Courts. The BBC in Seymour Road started their new Spotlight programme, there was a new £5 in circulation, and car number plates took on a new look with "A" appearing at the end of all new registrations. The Conservatives captured the City Council and Argyle were knocked out of the League Cup (6-0) at the first hurdle for the second season running by West Ham. Similarly West Bromwich Albion unceremoniously (5-1) ended Argyle's FA Cup dreams for the second time in four years, also at the first fence, in front of a 22,000-crowd at Home Park.

The New PLYMOUTH ZOO in Central Park

- Large Collection of Animals in Modern and Picturesque Setting of Gardens and Lawns
- Children's Amusements

Open every day of the year 10 a.m. to dusk

- Areas for Picnics etc.
- Refreshments
- Large Car Park

Admission
ADULTS 1/6
CHILDREN 1/-
Under 3 years - no charge

1964

The Harvest Home was pulled down, followed shortly afterwards by the Sugar Refinery and the Revenue, at either end of the doomed Duke Street. The short-lived roundabout at the end of Mutley Plain was replaced with traffic lights and Devonport (King's Road) Station was closed to passenger trains. The link between St Budeaux (Victoria Road) and Devonport Junction also closed. Former Plymouth MP Nancy Astor died and the Ford Palladium cinema closed. Seaton Barracks was extensively rebuilt and parts of the dockyard were bridged. Edwin Beckley retired and sold John Yeo's to Debenhams. St Paul's Church at Efford was completed and it was said that since 1951 some 4,652 houses had been built in Plympton and Plymstock. The city's overall housing target had been passed with 2,250 prefabs, which they were beginning to replace. Some 13,542 permanent council homes had been built, 853 Admiralty homes and 3,586 private houses, bringing the total to over 20,000. With Beatlemania still dominating the pop and non-pop headlines, the fab foursome paid two visits to the city, packing out the ABC Cinema, a venue used by many top pop package tours. Plymouth Argyle, who narrowly missed relegation, played Huddersfield six times this season, twice in the league, once in the FA Cup and three times in the league cup. Three games were drawn, the others all lost.

O·B
HARVEST
HOME

BEATLES

LOOK WESTWARD
JUNE 14–20
6d
Ready Steady Win!
NEW FACES, OLD FAVOURITES
See Pages 6-7

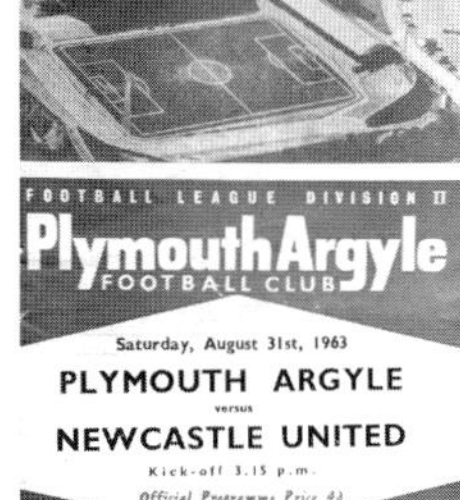
FOOTBALL LEAGUE DIVISION II
Plymouth Argyle
FOOTBALL CLUB
Saturday, August 31st, 1963
PLYMOUTH ARGYLE
versus
NEWCASTLE UNITED
Kick-off 3.15 p.m.
Official Programme Price 4d.
SAFELY ENTRUST ALL YOUR ELECTRICAL REQUIREMENTS TO
MADGE & SON
PORTLAND SQUARE PLYMOUTH Tel. 63315

Christmas
CHEER

LYMOUTH SCOUTS
GANG SHOW 1964
30th MARCH - 4th APRIL

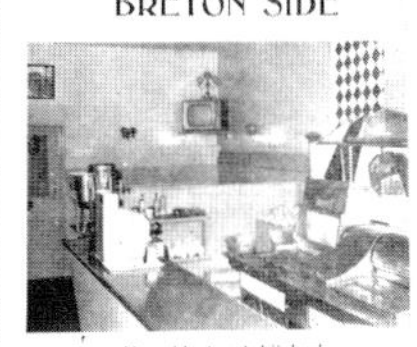
J. ANTONUCCI
BRETON SIDE
The oldest established
FISH AND CHIP SHOP
in Plymouth
Only best quality sold
Seating accommodation
PAY US A VISIT

PLYMOUTH
PROFILE

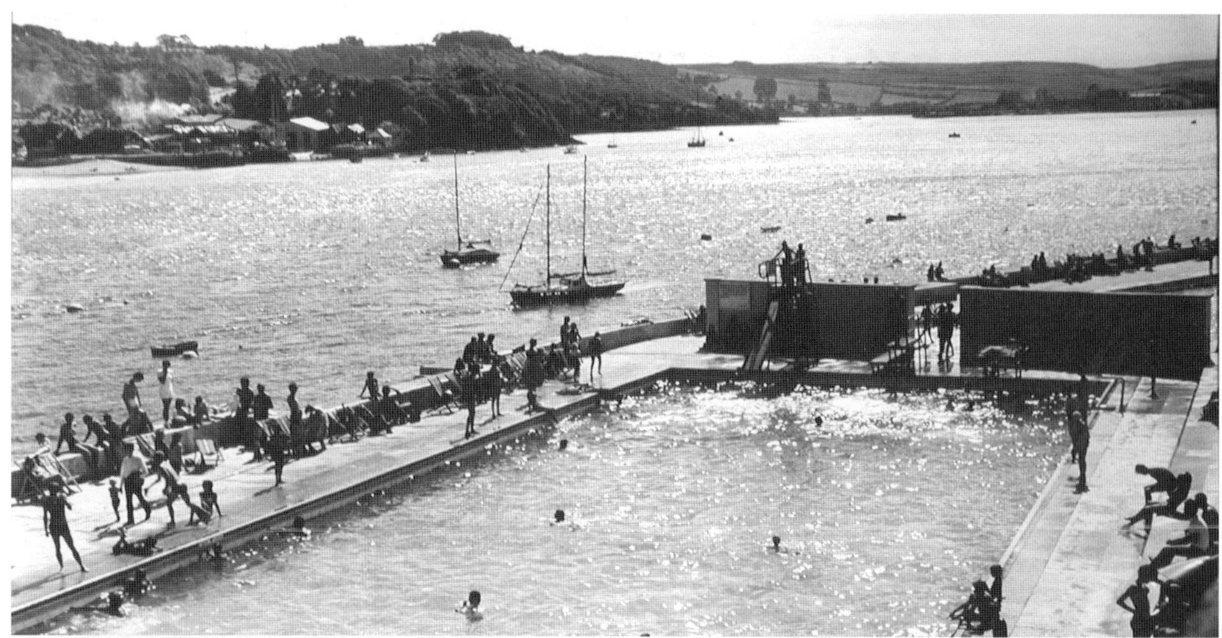

Plymouth's swimmers had never had it so good - first the indoor pool at the Ballard Centre and now the new Central Park Pool, added to which were the existing outdoor facilities at Mount Wise and Tinside. Just above Tinside the Mallard Cafe opened in April, while further up on the Hoe, at the end of the promenade, the Grand Hotel was relaunched as a Berni Inn - grilled rump steak at 11/6d. On 12 June the main hall of the new Blindman's Wood Scout headquarters was opened and the following month Westward TV announced a trading profit of £293,803. Peter Cadbury, the chairman, said that copyright of Gus Honeybun was vested in a subsidiary company - Torcliff. The folk music scene locally was blossoming with Cyril Tawney one of the principal players. One of the key players with Argyle was centre forward Frank Lord who scored six goals in the club's great run in the league cup which ended one step short of Wembley when they lost 1-0 to Leicester City at Home Park, having gone down 3-2 in the away leg. Leicester, winners the previous season, lost to Chelsea 3-2 in the two-legged final. Coincidentally Leicester also knocked the Pilgrims out of the FA Cup. *Show Boat* was the Carmenians' big production, the Tamaritans staged *Blithe Spirit*, the *Rehearsal* and the *Glass Menagerie*, and the Plymouth Amateur Operatic Society put on *Call Me Madam* at the Palace Theatre.

WESTWARD TELEVISION

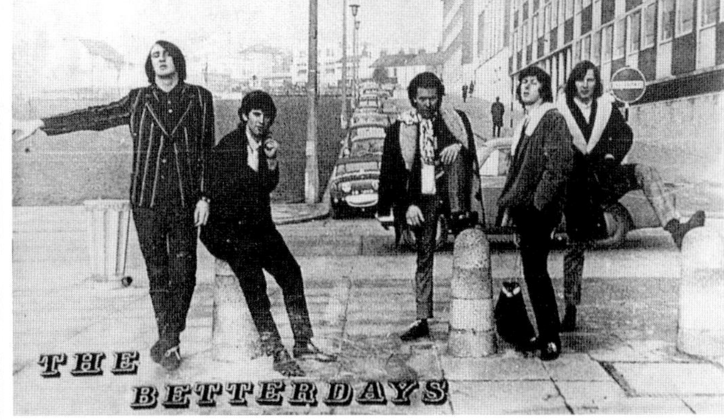
THE
BETTERDAYS

MAX FACTOR
2/9
BUYS!
7d

CAPSTAN
689

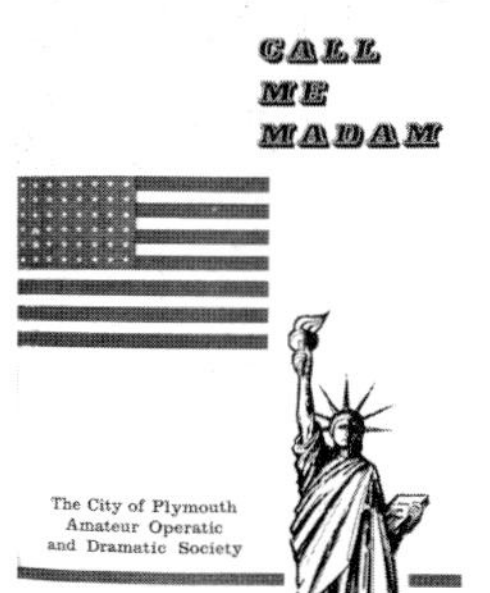
CALL
ME
MADAM
The City of Plymouth
Amateur Operatic
and Dramatic Society
PALACE THEATRE
PLYMOUTH
3 - 8 MAY 1965

PLYMOUTH ARGYLE
FOOTBALL CLUB
1529
P.A.F.C

PLYMOUTH
MODERN CITY OF THE WEST
CENTRE OF A 100 TOURS

HOE THEATRE
EDWARD KENT presents
Starlight
Rendezvous
THE
SCINTILLATING
SUMMER
SHOW
6d
SOUVENIR PROGRAMME
Christmas
CHEER
1965
Plymouth's own magazine

Drake's Circus Roundabout started to take shape. The Victorian Technical College had gone and the new Technical College was expanding. For Second Division Plymouth Argyle the season's highlights included two hat-tricks, one by the former milkman Mike Bickle in the 6-0 FA Cup mauling of non-league Corby Town, the other from Gunnislake-born Mike Trebilcock earlier in the season when the Pilgrims thrashed Birmingham City 6-1 at Home Park. Everton paid £23,000 for Trebilcock on 1st January 1966 and the young Cornishman rewarded them with the two goals that put Everton back on level terms with Sheffield Wednesday in the FA Cup Final and contributed largely to their 3-2 victory. England won the World Cup at Wembley thanks to another hat-trick - from Geoff Hurst, who later that year paraded the Jules Rimet trophy at Home Park with fellow West Ham and England stars, Martin Peters and Bobby Moore, as the English League played a representative Irish League side. England won 12-1 in front of a full house. Meanwhile there was a World Semi-Final battled out at Pennycross Stadium as Johnny Marquand won through to the Speedway Final in which he would also succeed. David Owen, son of a Plympton doctor, was elected MP for Sutton.

TARGET
FRIDAY
GIRLS!
GO
TARGET
FASHION
OPENS
POLICE
POLICE
Plymouth 1966
Navy Days
PLYMOUTH ARGYLE
FOOTBALL CLUB
1898
P.A.F.C.
PLYMOUTH
MODERN CITY OF THE WEST
WORLD
CHAMPIONSHIP
SEMI-FINAL
present
UNDER
MILK
WOOD
BY DYLAN THOMAS

1967

An enormous crowd struggled to see much when the lone-round-the-world yachtsman, Francis Chichester, completed his epic journey, landing at dusk at the Royal Western Yacht Club on 28 May. The Crown & Anchor on the Barbican was later renamed the Sir Francis Chichester in his honour and the Hoe Park Hotel became the Gypsy Moth IV, after his boat. Another sea-going vessel in the national and local news was the stricken tanker *Torrey Canyon* which spilled an 18-mile-long oil slick off the coast of Cornwall. The Government extended territorial fishing waters to 12 miles and Sutton Harbour planned to modernise the Fish Quay. The Barbican, meanwhile, was designated only the second conservation area in the country. Cattedown power station switched from sea-borne to rail-borne coal while a new gas plant, using oil distillate, opened in the old Breakwater Quarry at Pomphlett. Plymouth's boundaries were extended to incorporate Plympton and Plymstock and the new roundabout at Manadon was completed. The left tower of the Royal Albert Gate at Keyham was pulled down, the eight-storey block of the Technical College was completed, and there was a farewell parade for more than 300 members of Plymouth City Police as it became part of a new and larger unit - Devon and Cornwall. Cricket legend Gary Sobers played here with the International Cricket Crusaders.

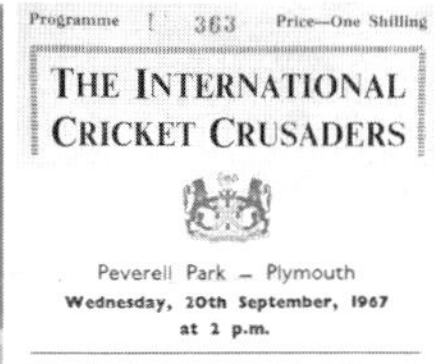

Programme 363 Price—One Shilling

THE INTERNATIONAL CRICKET CRUSADERS

Peverell Park – Plymouth
Wednesday, 20th September, 1967
at 2 p.m.

The Tour Fixtures and Dates

Sat.	Sept. 16th	Cornish Crusaders XI at Helston	2 p.m.
Sun.	Sept. 17th	Wadebridge at Wadebridge	12 noon
Tues.	Sept. 19th	Callington at Callington	2 p.m.
Wed.	Sept. 20th	Plymouth at Peverell Park, Plymouth	2 p.m.
Thurs.	Sept. 21st	Brixham at Brixham	2 p.m.
Sat.	Sept. 23rd	North Devon at Instow	12 noon
Sun.	Sept. 24th	Exmouth at Exmouth	12 noon

BOWDEN (SPORTS) LTD.
ATLANTIC BUILDING
51 MAYFLOWER STREET PLYMOUTH
WE SPECIALIZE IN THE BEST EQUIPMENT
FOR ALL SPORTS AND INDOOR GAMES
PLYMOUTH CRICKET CLUB, ARGYLE, SCHOOLS AND SERVICE UNITS

1968

The Duke of Edinburgh visited the Tecalemit factory, Sutton MP David Owen was appointed Navy Minister in the Labour Government, and Robert Daniel became the new chairman of Plymouth Argyle. A two-tier postal system was introduced - 5d and 4d - both up from the old 3d rate. The old shilling and the two-bob bit were replaced by the new 5p and 10p. No 19 Group RAF Coastal Command left Mount Batten, and Drake's Island, which had been a rat-infested site a few years ago, was now a thriving youth centre. There was a new youth centre at Plympton too. Argyle had a thoroughly dismal time, managing only nine wins all season in the league and both cups. Not surprisingly, they were relegated. However they did do the double over Aston Villa. A season ticket for the 1968/9 Third Division campaign would cost you £8.8.0. for a seat in the centre of the grandstand. Work began on the new 104-bedroom Mayflower Hotel on The Hoe and an extension was built for the School of Maritime Studies at Portland Square. In May, Plymouth competed with Torbay on The Hoe for the BBC TV show It's A Knockout, with the prospect of taking a 20-strong team of youngsters for the second round in Belgium at stake. The Pussycat Club in the Palace Theatre became well-known for its exotic dancers, while Plymouth's cinemas looked increasingly to X-rated films for their continued survival.

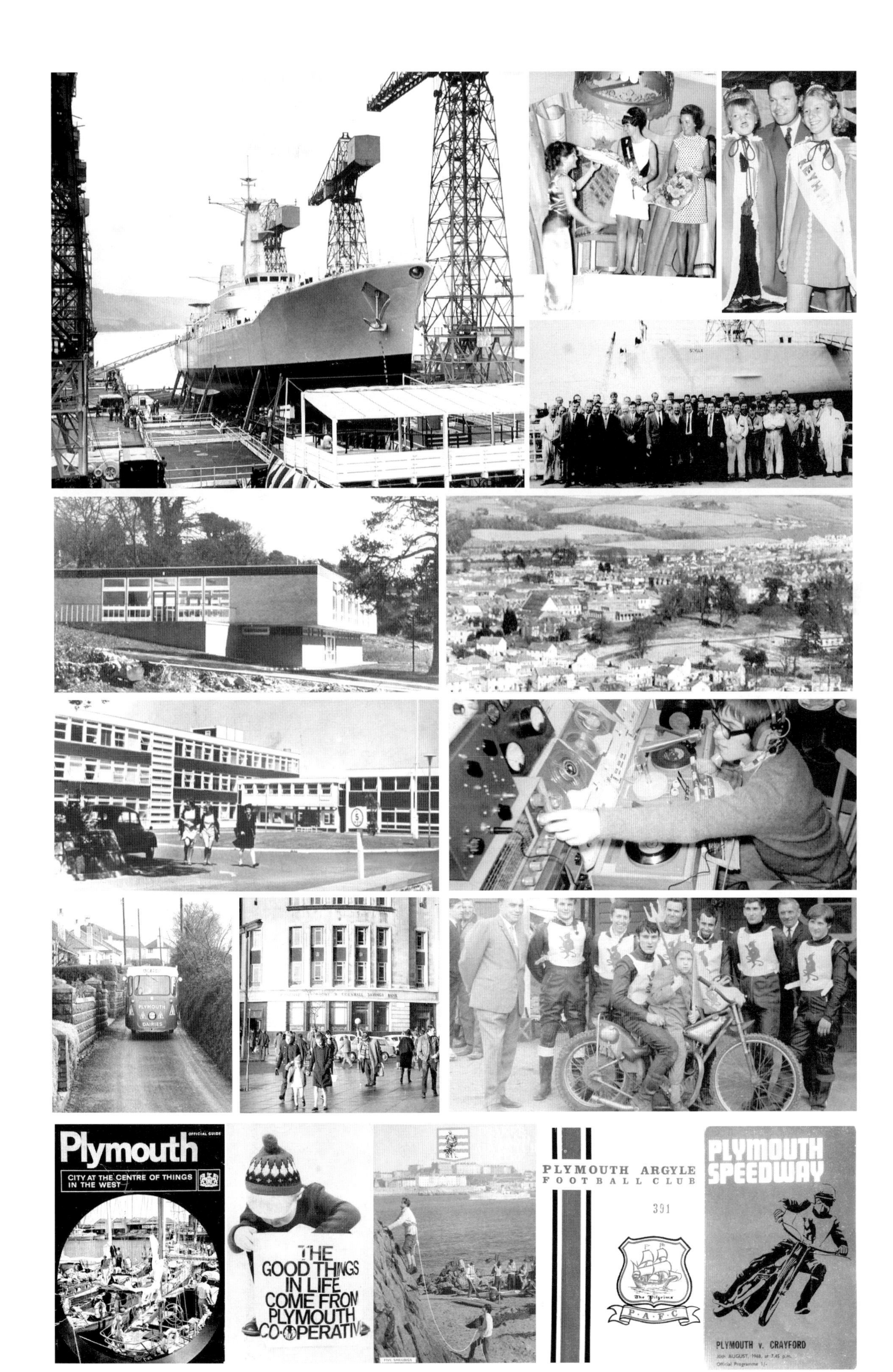
Plymouth
OFFICIAL GUIDE
CITY AT THE CENTRE OF THINGS IN THE WEST
THE GOOD THINGS IN LIFE COME FROM PLYMOUTH CO-OPERATIVE
PLYMOUTH ARGYLE FOOTBALL CLUB
391
P.A.F.C.
PLYMOUTH SPEEDWAY
PLYMOUTH v. CRAYFORD
PLYMOUTH DAIRIES

1969

It was announced in June that a new 464-acre suburb would be built in Leigham/Estover. "The area, separated from the rest of the city by Forder Valley, can be planned to give a sense of unity." Raglan Barracks and Pomphlett Mill were both demolished, the coal-powered plant at Coxside Gasworks was closed, and Plymouth was granted intermediate "development area" status. Dr David Owen, Navy Minister and MP for Sutton, announced plans to develop a new operational base at Devonport for nuclear-powered fleet submarines. Colour television finally arrived in the City. The old halfpenny ceased to be legal tender and the ten shilling note was replaced by a strange-shaped 50p coin. Many Mutley residents were unhappy at the proposal to spend £140,000 on a three-storey car park over a railway cutting between Ermington Terrace and Napier Terrace. Meanwhile the Western College Players staged *Boeing Boeing* at the Athenaeum, the De Silva Puppet Company put on *Jack And The Beanstalk* at the Hoe Theatre, and the Carmenians' annual showpiece was *The Desert Song*. The City of Plymouth Amateur Operatic & Dramatic Society staged the *Pyjama Game*. Unfortunately, third Division Argyle failed to score in any of the three league cup encounters with Fourth Division Exeter City. The second of the replays was played at Plainmoor, Torquay's ground.

ABC PLYMOUTH
SUNDAY JANUARY 4th
FOR 7 DAYS
JOHN WAYNE GLEN CAMPBELL KIM DARBY
HAL WALLIS' PRODUCTION TRUE GRIT.

THE PAJAMA GAME
POPS HOUSE
THE OPORTO

Stuart Hutchison

FORTE'S
car park

JOHN BULL INTERNATIONAL
FEB. 6-8
38 LODGE ST. TEL. PLYMOUTH 60060

PLYMOUTH
ZOO

PLYMOUTH ARGYLE
FOOTBALL CLUB

The Pilgrims
P.A.F.C

PLYMOUTH
Speedway
CHALLENGE MATCH
PLYMOUTH v EASTBOURNE
PLYMOUTH SPORTS STADIUM
GOOD FRIDAY APRIL 4 1969 AT 3.35 p.m.
1969 SEASON
MEETING No. 1
1/-

"I'm a Turner's fan —
They always play the game"
UP THE ARGYLE!
AUSTIN HOUSE

Turners
Austin House · Derrys Cross · Plymouth 62333
· AUSTIN & VANDEN PLAS DISTRIBUTORS ·
· RILEY RETAIL DEALERS ·
Quality Used Cars!

MON SEPT 1st BANK HOLIDAY '69
POP & BLUES FESTIVAL
PENNYCROSS STADIUM
PLYMOUTH
2PM-8PM 6 HOURS OF TOP STAR GROUPS
FLEETWOOD MAC
THE MOVE
GENO WASHINGTON & THE RAM JAM BAND
NASHVILLE TEENS * DAVE AMBOY
The ROD MASON JASS BAND
* COMPERES *
ANDY PRICE · COLIN (READY STEADY) EDDIE
DOORS OPEN 12 NOON
Tickets 20/- EACH

1970

On 1 January Plymouth Polytechnic came into being and at the same time the College of Further Education was created. There were great celebrations for the 350th anniversary of the sailing of the Mayflower. About 60,000 people were on The Hoe when Senator Leverett Saltonstall (a descendant of a Pilgrim Father) launched Mayflower 70. The £700,000 Mayflower Hotel was also opened, as was the Holiday Inn on the edge of Armada Way. New accommodation blocks also appeared at HMS *Drake* but the Royal Navy, across the board, ended its age-old issuing of a tot of rum. Officials in Plymouth and London expanded an overspill agreement whereby new firms were encouraged to come down here - among them Wrigleys, Die Casting Machine Tools, Rodene Timber, D O & E Industries and Arrow Electrics. Plans were drawn up to build another 10,000 homes over the next ten years. The first section of North Cross Roundabout was completed - the Ministry of Transport contributed £566,438. The half-crown and 10/- note ceased to be legal tender and Ted Heath ended Labour's run - but there were no changes in Plymouth - Joan Vickers (Dev) and David Owen (Sut). After the refit of *Ark Royal*, Owen announced plans to cover the Yard's three dry docks. Charlie Chester spent the summer in the Hoe Theatre and a Bavarian-style Bier Keller opened in Union Street.

COLLEGE OF ART
Hawkins
Magnet

POST OFFICE
MARTIN

Goodbodys
Catering
THE ROOF DECK RESTAURANT
CIVIC CENTRE BUILDING
Visit also our
RESTAURANTS and SNACK BARS at
38, ROYAL PARADE
49, MUTLEY PLAIN

Track
Record
Smashed
Today?
PLYMOUTH
SPEEDWAY
REVIEW
GOOD FRIDAY, MARCH 27, 1970
EASTBOURNE
EAGLES

The family size family like this shops at Dingles. There they find good value for money, good quality, friendly service, and reliability. All at Dingles. Depend on Dingles and all shop happily ever after
dp Dingles dp
of Plymouth
ROYAL PARADE · PLYMOUTH · Tel. 66811

1970
Plymouth Welcomes Pilgrims
and holiday-makers too!

MAYFLOWER '70
1620-1970
Come to the Westcountry in 1970
An exciting programme of events has been arranged to celebrate the sailing of the Pilgrim Fathers

Duke of Cornwall
Plymouth's Finest Hotel
AA • RAC
You will find all that you want from a three-star hotel at the Duke of Cornwall, Plymouth. Central location near the Hoe and City Centre shops. Private suites, lifts to all floors and radio in all rooms. Luxurious restaurant and banqueting suites with superb cuisine and imaginative wine cellar. Ballroom - public dances each Wednesday and Saturday. Cocktail bar and Clan bar. Fully licensed. Centrally heated. Television lounges. Located in the Hotel Cellars, 'The Spider's Web' - a different lounge bar and eating-house that provides selected Aberdeen-Angus steaks and a full à la carte menu from 6.30 p.m.
Telephone 0752 66256 [illegible]
Telegrams: 'Dukotel'
Managing Director
L. McDERMOTT-BROWN, [illegible]

1971

Britain went decimal: the old threepenny bit bit the dust and into our pockets and purses came the new 1p, and 2p. The tills at Tozers stopped ringing as the only major Devonport store to move into Plymouth after the war closed down and Dingles was taken over by the House of Fraser. The pedestrian shopping complex at Drake Circus was completed and the College of St Mark & St John moved down here from Chelsea. The last goods trains pulled out of Devonport (King's Road) Station and the green light was given for a new College of Further Education to be built on the site. The last of the quayside railways, which had serviced Stonehouse, Sutton Harbour and Millbay, were also all closed now. The Garrison Church of St Alban's, Crownhill, shut as the last infantry battalion marched out of Plymouth. Plans for a massive new power station at Insworke were well under way and the Crabtree Inn was pulled down to make way for the new dual carriageway. The *Kathleen & May* arrived in Sutton Harbour; the Duke of Edinburgh, who had been instrumental in its preservation, was among the first visitors; and Robert Lenkiewicz, who had come to Plymouth four years earlier, was working on a 50ft by 40ft Barbican mural showing a group of Elizabethans walking through an alleyway. Plymouth was demoted as a local authority and Southway was made a separate parish.

IT'S
A
MANS
CASUAL
WORLD
AT
JOHN
CONWAY
SHOPS FOR MEN
81 Cornwall St., Plymouth
Exeter & Torquay.

NO ENTRY

ROD MASON JASS BAND

Gentleman of Stratford
presented by THE CARMENIANS

WELCOME TO PLYMOUTH
NOW VISIT
Louis Boutique
MAN SHOP
For something different in
Men's Wear
MANS SHOP
Louis Boutique

PLYMOUTH
Holiday City
by the sea
bounded by
the Dartmoor
National Park

JUST FOR THE RECORD.....
City Radio
have an excellent
selection of Popular, Jazz and Classical 45's
EP's and LP's for your leisure enjoyment.
Visit our Record Department and consult
for your record requirements.
Stockists of
Columbia - Decca - EMI - HMV - MGM - Parlophone -
Polydor - Philips - PYE - RCA Victor -
Regal Zonophone - Stax - Tamla Motown.
CITY RADIO

ALL OUR RECORDS ARE GROOVY
JAZZ
folk
black and white is beautiful
Do Not Collect £200
WOW!
COOL
peter russell's hot record store ltd.

Holiday Inn
Stay at the best hotel in Plymouth

1972

The first girls were admitted to Tamar High School as it became the city's first co-educational grammar school. Outside it, work was almost complete on infilling a section of the creek between Stonehouse Bridge and Millbridge. St Joseph's Primary School in Raglan Road had its first intake of pupils, Plymouth's Law Courts became home to the newly-created Plymouth Crown Court, and work began on the restoration of the Merchant's House. Brymon Airways began operating at Roborough, and Sutton Harbour established a new marina off North Quay. Hermon Terrace (Outland Road) was demolished to make room for the new dual carriageway down to Manadon, and two Southern Railway bridges - over Wolseley Road at St Budeaux and Weston Mill - were pulled down. At Home Park, Bertie Mee's Arsenal appeared in October for a testimonial match to honour goalkeeping legend and Home Park stalwart Bill Harper. Bob Wilson and Charlie George were among the Gunners' squad. Hailed as one of Britain's most advanced office buildings, the new £900,000 accounting base of the South Western Electricity Board opened in Outland Road with £1 million of complex computer equipment. Lord Mayor Dorothy Innes toured the premises with senior council officials. Meanwhile, on the buses, the Corporation banned smoking on its single-decker, one-man-operated vehicles.

Togs for Lively Lads
Head into Hornes for the liveliest boys' outfits in town. Suits, knitwear, casual jackets and slacks—they're all there, ready and waiting for you to try them on.
HORNES
TODAY'S TOP SHOP FOR BOYS WEAR
HORNE BROTHERS, 44 NEW GEORGE STREET, PLYMOUTH

CONTINENTAL HOTEL
MILLBAY ROAD PLYMOUTH Tel 20782
5p
No 1
PRESENT
TAVERN IN THE TOWN**
The New SUMMER SHOW!
AT THE FRIENDLIEST PLACE IN TOWN!

Fun bug
2 aircraft seats.
Lift-up, aircraft-type cockpit cover.
Rustproof body.
Most exciting new car idea in years!
J.A. Blonden (MOTORS) LTD.
We've got the BOND BUG
Come and see it!
102 VAUXHALL ST.
BARBICAN
PLYMOUTH.
Telephone: 65152
PLYMOUTH'S MAIN AGENTS

JERRY JEROME presents
GORDON PETERS
in
The HOE SHOW '72
AT THE HOE THEATRE PLYMOUTH

PLYMOUTH ARGYLE
The Bill Harper Testimonial Match
TUESDAY, OCTOBER 17th, 1972
Kick-off 7.30 p.m.
ARSENAL

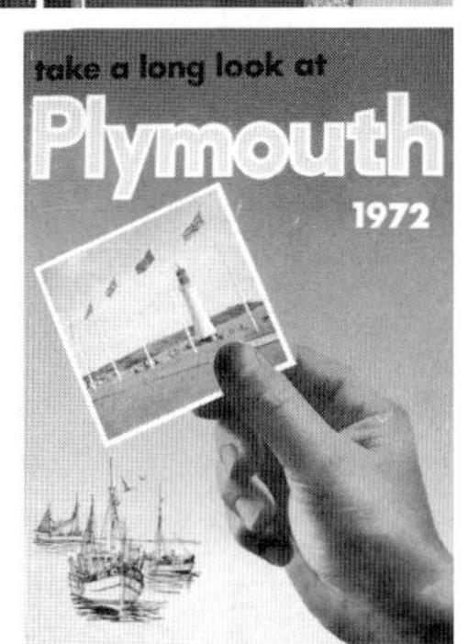
take a long look at
Plymouth
1972

1973

It's 7am on 3 January and the French ferry ship *Kerisnel* drops her stern door at Millbay and opens Plymouth's door to the EEC. The first vehicle ashore brought cauliflowers from Brittany. The 200-berth Ocean Quay Marina was opened at Richmond Walk with 82 luxury flats, the Kitto Centre at Burrington provided the city with a new indoor sports facility, and the Armada Way subway under Royal Parade was completed. The dual carriageway along the Embankment came into service and the city became the base of the Royal Marine Commandos with their HQ at Mount Wise and men at Stonehouse, Seaton, Bickleigh and the Citadel. The BBC local radio programme Morning Sou'West first hit the air and it was announced that the first phase of Derriford Hospital would begin in 15 months. Dutch Elm disease put 8,000 trees in the city at risk; many were lost in Central Park. At Home Park an Under-23 England International was played. Plymouth-born Birmingham City player Trevor Francis appeared alongside Argyle's Colin Sullivan and Arsenal's Ray Kennedy and Charlie George. Firms looking for staff included Texas Instruments and Farleys. Average earnings for a young woman packing baby food were £20 a week for a day shift (6.55am-4.25pm) and £9 part-time. Ivor Emmanuel was in the Hoe Summer Show and *Orpheus In The Underworld* was the Carmenians' offering.

Babes in the Wood
HOE THEATRE, PLYMOUTH

CHARLES HARDING

WHITBREAD

"Who says the Bible is dull?"
"AS ACCORDING TO KOSSOFF"
DAVID KOSSOFF'S EVENING OF HIS T.V. & RADIO BIBLE STORES
"Hypnotic..Funny..Magic."
FOR ONE PERFORMANCE ONLY
20th APRIL 1973

OFFICIAL PROGRAMME 5p
PLYMOUTH ARGYLE
ASSOCIATION FOOTBALL CLUB
TESTIMONIAL MATCH
PLYMOUTH ARGYLE
MANCHESTER CITY
SOUVENIR PROGRAMME

the CARMENIANS present
Charlie Girl
CG1973
2nd APRIL TO 14th APRIL 1973

PLYMOUTH ARGYLE
SEASON 1972-73
WEDNESDAY, MARCH 14, 1973
Kick-off 7.30 p.m.
SANTOS of BRAZIL

ORPHEUS IN THE UNDERWORLD
Presented by THE CARMENIANS

OFFICIAL PROGRAMME
10p
ENGLAND v POLAND
UNDER 23 INTERNATIONAL
Home Park, Plymouth
Tuesday 16th October
Kick-off 7.30 pm

1974

The new College of Further Education was almost complete, groundwork began on Derriford Hospital and it was finally agreed that Roborough Airport could be improved. The Breakwater Fort Signal Station, closed four years earlier, was given a new role as a training base for divers. In Parliament Plymouth regained its third seat - Drake - and Janet Fookes won it for the Tories. David Owen moved from Sutton to Devonport and Alan Clark (Con) succeeded him in Sutton. In July, for the first time ever, the greatest cycling race in the World, the Tour de France, left the Continent and came to Plymouth. Belgian Eddy Merckx won the race for a second time but, locally and nationally, it was deemed to be a financial flop. In August, Spotlight South West, the early evening programme broadcast from the BBC's Seymour Road studios, went out in colour for the first time. Mother's Pride Bakery took over the 32 Goodbody shops in Plymouth, Devon and Cornwall, following the latter's collapse, and the future of Sunblest and Vitbe was in the balance.The City of Plymouth Amateur Operatic Society celebrated its 75th anniversary, and the Royal Ballet came to the Big Top in Central Park. There were exciting times for Argyle in both cups, losing 1-0 to Manchester United in the FA Cup and 3-1 (on aggregate) to Manchester City in the two-legged semi-final of the League Cup.

INTERNATIONAL MENSWEAR
Louis
INTERNATIONAL
57 CORNWALL STREET PLYMOUTH

ON RECORD
at City Radio
If you think carefully about buying records and naturally want to ponder over the best selection in Plymouth, then drop into City Radio. There, you will be able to find anything from Pop to Classical LP's to suit all tastes — and if you're stuck for that certain record, then with the expert advice of City Radio's record staff, you will be sure to go home with a very happy choice.
Just some of our features include — Greatest Hit LP Albums, Classical Record Sets, Folk (Traditional and Contemporary) LP's plus Films and Shows Soundtracks and Budget Albums (from 71p). For the children we have many Disney-Land LP's including "Robin Hood". Also a fine selection of Cassettes and Cartridges, (including the new classical sets — 3).
What more can we say except use your head!
CR
CITY RADIO
Colour Television Specialists
Radio & HiFi Equipment
Mutley Plain PLYMOUTH 64477

THE KNIT IN

ROYAL BALLET

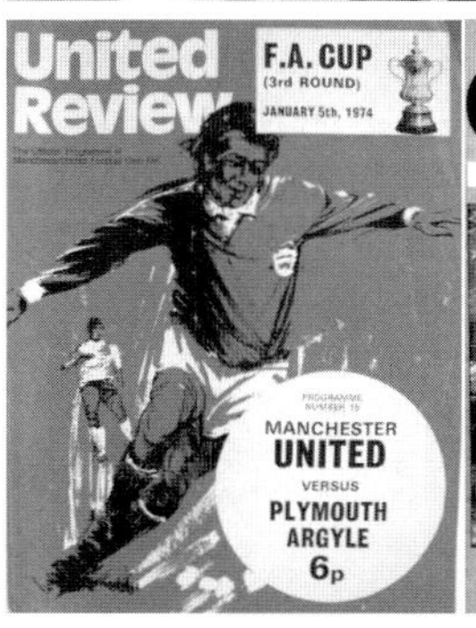
United Review
F.A. CUP
(3rd ROUND)
JANUARY 5th, 1974
MANCHESTER
UNITED
VERSUS
PLYMOUTH
ARGYLE
6p

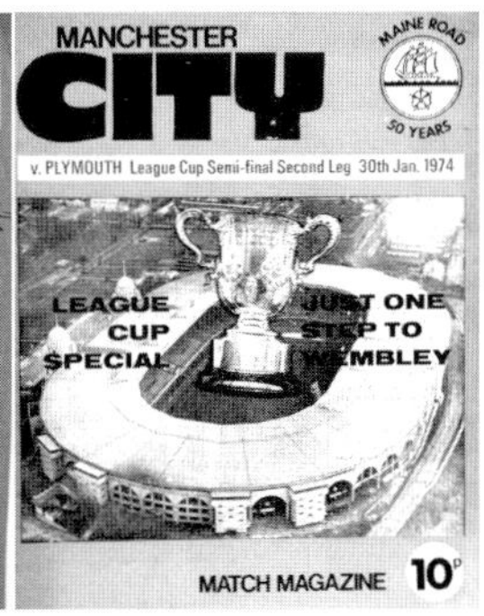
MANCHESTER
CITY
MAINE ROAD
50 YEARS
v. PLYMOUTH League Cup Semi-final Second Leg 30th Jan. 1974
LEAGUE CUP SPECIAL
JUST ONE STEP TO WEMBLEY
MATCH MAGAZINE 10p

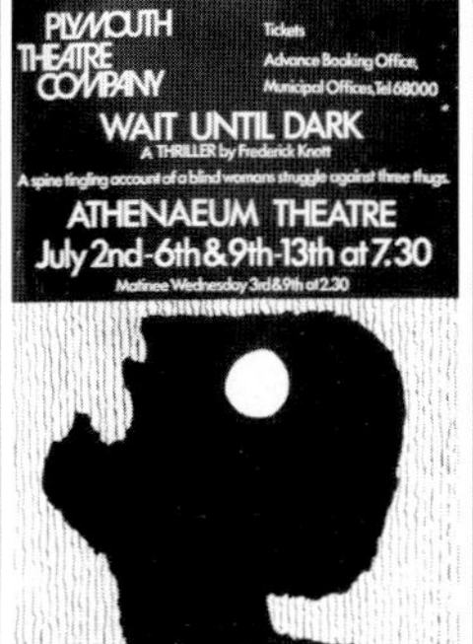
PLYMOUTH THEATRE COMPANY
Tickets
Advance Booking Office,
Municipal Offices, Tel 68000
WAIT UNTIL DARK
A THRILLER by Frederick Knott
A spine tingling account of a blind womans struggle against three thugs.
ATHENAEUM THEATRE
July 2nd-6th & 9th-13th at 7.30
Matinee Wednesday 3rd & 9th at 2.30

HOE THEATRE
PLYMOUTH
JOHN REDGRAVE, BY ARRANGEMENT WITH H.T.V. WEST AND ROY WARD DICKSON
PRESENTS
T.V'S
Most Popular Husband & Wife Quiz Game
MR & MRS

HOE THEATRE
PLYMOUTH THEATRE COMPANY PRESENTS
THE PANTOMIME
ALADDIN
and his wonderful lamp
THURS. 26th, DEC
TO SAT. 1st FEB. '75

1975

The railway embankment from North Road to Millbay was removed, paving the way for development on the western side of Western Approach. Mount Edgcumbe became a country park, to be jointly administered by Plymouth City and Cornwall County Councils. The restaurant at the top of the Civic Centre was closed on public safety grounds; offering stunning views of the city, it was only ever added on as an afterthought. England's smallest radio station, Plymouth Sound, began broadcasting from its Earl's Acre studios; David Bassett had a two hour Phone Forum in the morning and there were two hours of Talk With Louise (Churchill) in the afternoon. Carmella McKenzie had the drive-time slot. Budshead Manor barn was gutted by fire and there were fears about impact of the proposed redevelopment of the Pennycross Stadium site. The Swan Hotel, Devonport, closed for a number of months, was re-opened as one of the area's first real ale pubs, and suddenly Plymouth found itself with two new wine bars - Dudleys and Oysters - both on the Barbican. Argyle had one of their best seasons in years, achieving promotion to Division II and enjoying another good cup run, this time in the FA Cup, losing 3-1 to Everton in the 4th round in front of 38,000 at Home Park. Paul Mariner and Billy Rafferty were the focal point of the attack, both netting more than 20 league goals.

DINE OUT AT
THE CHINA GARDEN
Plymouth's most Luxurious Restaurant
頤和酒家
Open noon to 11.30 p.m.
(including Sundays)
Fully licensed. Parties catered for.
17–19 DERRY'S CROSS • PLYMOUTH 64472.
ADJACENT TO WESTWARD TELEVISION.

PLYMOUTH
ANCIENT PORT MODERN RESORT

the pilgrim

RAIN SAVED PLAY!
Pitch expert now admits: The bad summer was good for Argyle

PLYMOUTH THEATRE COMPANY
Plymouth's Professional Theatre Company
presents
CANDIDA
by
BERNARD SHAW
HOE THEATRE
5th Nov until 15th Nov at 7.30.
Matinee Wed 12th at 2.30.
On Tour, 17th Nov until 13th Dec.
(no Monday performances)

The Carmenians
25th
THE MERRY WIDOW

HOE THEATRE
Cinderella
FRI. 26th. DEC –
SAT. 31st. JAN '76
10p

Brymon Airways laid their first tarmac runway at Roborough, Marine Projects took over the Plympton factory of Hurley Marine, and the last of Plymouth's flour mills - Spillers' Valletort Mill - shut. It was a bit of a bombshell for most of their 200 employees. The Duke of Edinburgh opened the Library, Learning Resources and Students' Union Buildings of Plymouth Polytechnic, and work began on the demolition of Nazareth House, the old Edgcumbe Winter villa overlooking Firestone Bay, Stonehouse. Plymouth guest-house landlady, Beryl Cook, made her London gallery debut following her sell-out first show at Plymouth Arts Centre last year. The Foots Barn Theatre Company staged their panto *Beauty And The Beast* in Charles-with-St Matthias church hall and Plymouth Theatre Company put on *Cinderella* in the Hoe Theatre. Snobs, Tiffs and Fiesta were popular disco venues, and EMI announced that the ABC cinema would follow the Drake by converting to three screens. Opened with a seating capacity of 2,400, the new screens would seat 378, 367, and 125. The stalls were to be adapted as a 1,200-seater bingo hall. The last live event with the old layout was the Morecambe & Wise Show - and every seat was sold. Plymouth's new divisional police headquarters at Crownhill became operational when staff took over from their colleagues at the old Greenbank Station.

Match Programme and
Official Club Newspaper of Plymouth Argyle

The Pilgrim

Support Argyle Now and it could be a case of

YOU LUCKY PEOPLE!

INSIDE

TONY WAITERS on 'Why we need Full Time Refs'

Paul Mariner Profile

Has Gough hit out once too often?

"HARPERS PARK"

BBC tv SPORTS SOUTH WEST

Council staff were given an extra day off for the Queen's Silver Jubilee. The Sex Pistols played Woods for a second time, Castaways was another popular live venue. Yeo's and Spooners were renamed Debenhams (the company had actually taken over Spooners in the 1920s and Yeo's in 1964) and the police moved into their new £1 million sub-divisional HQ at Charles Cross. In May, Plymouth was finally linked to the national motorway system. On 23 September Foreign Secretary David Owen opened the £1.75 million Institute for Marine Environmental Research and the following day he officated at the opening of Devonport Dockyard's new £18 million Frigate Complex. Plymouth's fishing fleet was up to 150 vessels and John Laing won the bid to build 407 new council homes at Estover - the second stage - at a cost of £3.6 million. There was a £1,000 top prize in the Plymouth Lottery and a family of four could visit Drake's Island for £1.40. The restored Merchant's House in St Andrew Street was opened, while the Central Hospital in Lockyer Street and the Methodist Church on Mutley Plain were closed. Argyle lost five of their last six matches, the other was a goal-less draw, and after just two seasons they once again dropped out of the Second Division. Earlier in the season they suffered the indignity of losing to 3rd Division Exeter City at home, and away, in the League Cup.

centenary
PLYMOTHIAN
1877
1977
SPEEDO

Plymouth
Price 25p

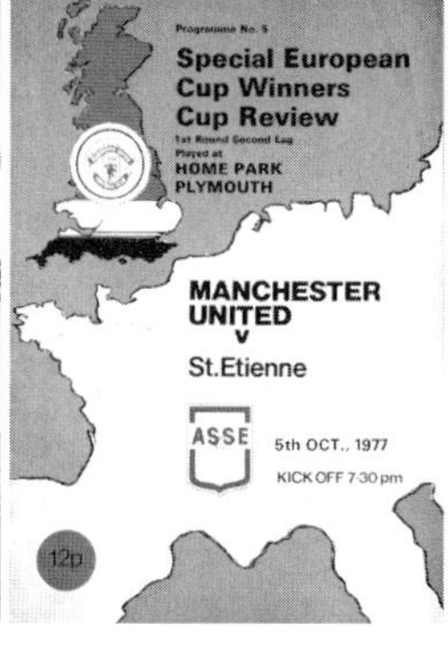

Programme No. 5
Special European
Cup Winners
Cup Review
1st Round Second Leg
Played at
HOME PARK
PLYMOUTH
MANCHESTER
UNITED
v
St.Etienne
ASSE
5th OCT., 1977
KICK OFF 7.30 pm
12p

PLYMOUTH
THEATRE
COMPANY
Plymouth's
Professional Theatre
Company
PORTRAIT OF A QUEEN
BY WILLIAM FRANCIS
ATHENAEUM THEATRE
8th Sept until 24th Sept at 7.30
Matinees Wed 14th and 21st at 2.30

PLYMOUTH
THEATRE
COMPANY
Plymouth's
Professional Theatre
Company
QUEEN ELIZABETH
SLEPT HERE ?
Athenaeum Theatre
June 23rd until July 9th at 7.30
Matinee Wed 29th and 6th at 2.30

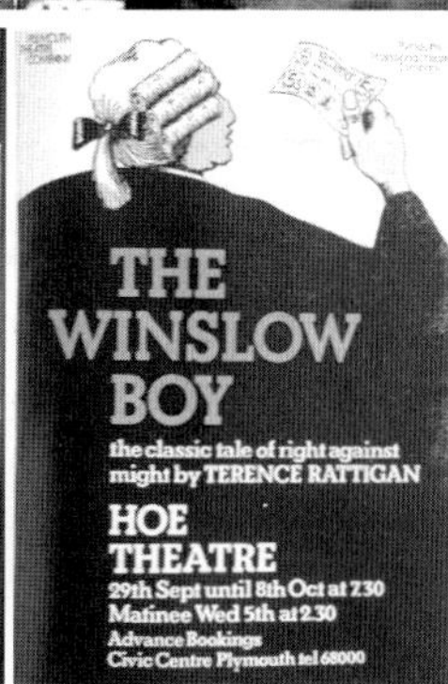

THE
WINSLOW
BOY
the classic tale of right against
might by TERENCE RATTIGAN
HOE
THEATRE
29th Sept until 8th Oct at 7.30
Matinee Wed 5th at 2.30
Advance Bookings
Civic Centre Plymouth tel 68000

1978

The *Ark Royal* returned and the *Eagle* departed - for burial in Loch Ryan. The annual Dockyard wage bill was over £50 million and Plymouth's population had grown to 259,000 - it had been 207,000 fifty years earlier. The acreage, meanwhile, had increased almost fourfold - from 5,711 to 20,000. Since the war the Council had built 21,000 houses and flats and there were a further 19,500 private dwellings. 50 new manufacturing industries and suppliers had settled here. Brymon Airways were now carrying 60,000 passengers a year and Brittany Ferries' figures were about to increase with the addition of the route to Santander. The *Kathleen & May* left Sutton Harbour for London, Costers closed down, following the retirement of Geoffrey Leatherby, and Energy Secretary Anthony Benn refused to approve plans for the power station at Insworke. Theatrical impressario John Redgrave revived the Palace Theatre, re-opening on Boxing Day with *Cinderella* - starring Frankie Howerd, Julian Orchard and John Boulter - while Malcolm Allison, sacked 13 years earlier, was brought back to Home Park to try to keep the Pilgrims out of the Fourth Division for the first time in their history. Seven goals in the last eleven games from striker Fred Binney helped them avoid the drop - just - but for the second consecutive season Exeter City knocked them out of the League Cup.

OPM CLUB
EFFORD LANE

NOVEMBER
3 QUARRY
4
10 BADGER
11
17 SPARE PARTS
18
24 Candlelight Supper
25
DECEMBER
1 GREASED LIGHTENING
2
8 QUARRY
9
15 BRICKS
16

Royal Opera House
Midland Bank
City of Plymouth
Sadler's Wells Royal Ballet in the 'Big Top'
Higher Home Park Plymouth
26 Jun - 15 Jul 1978

1979

Work began on the Peter Moro-designed Theatre Royal, and Prince Charles officiated at the opening of the Magistrates' Court in St Andrew Street. Tony Irish was the project architect, Cliff Moiser the Clerk to the Magistrates. 450 staff moved to the new £2 million Bowyers Factory on Newnham industrial estate and plans were unveiled for a 113-bed hotel on land adjacent to the Tecalemit site at Marsh Mills. The summer saw the city start to celebrate the 400th Anniversary of Drake's circumnavigation with an entertainment extravaganza in Central Park - Sam, the "smoking, organ-playing, bicycle-riding Rhesus monkey" and Dr Who's car were among the top attractions. Admission was £1. There was a Massed Military Bands Spectacular in the Citadel - tickets £2-3. Stebbing's Shoe Shop in Union Street closed after 109 years, and James Paton-Watson, joint-architect of the 1943 Plan for Plymouth, upon which the city centre was fairly faithfully modelled, died aged 81. Mutley Methodist Church was demolished and Belgrave Road was made one way for two weeks during the work. Joseph was at the Hoe Theatre and Fiona Richmond came to the New Palace Theatre. Argyle pulled a little clearer of the relegation zone; Fred Binney, Gary Megson and Brian Johnson were the leading scorers. Sadly, non-league Worcester City dumped the Pilgrims out of the FA Cup.

HOMECRAFT
FITTED FURNITURE SPECIALISTS
City Centre (A 386)
Car Park

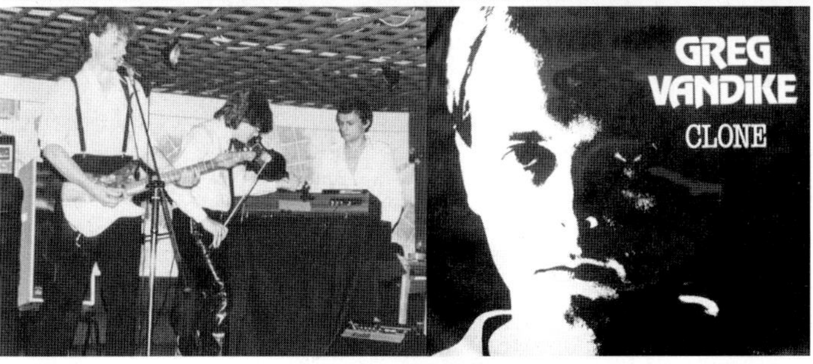
GREG
VANDIKE
CLONE

NEW
SUTTON
HARBOUR
REGATTA
1979
21ST - 28TH JULY 1979

Take time out ...
... to visit Holiday Inn

BEDROOM
FARCE
by
ALAN AYCKBOURN
PLYMOUTH ATHENÆUM THEATRE - JUNE 21 to JULY 14
1979

"YES
WE HAVE NO
PYJAMAS"

ARGYLE
THE OFFICIAL MATCH MAGAZINE OF PLYMOUTH ARGYLE FOOTBALL CLUB
Football League Division Three
Plymouth Argyle
v
Sheffield Wednesday

Emu at the Palace

Official Programme PLYMOUTH HOE THEATRE
Commencing Wed. 26th December 1979
How to get your man
JOSEPH
Hey Dreamer you'll make it
PHARAOH tells all!
MUGGED AND LEFT TO DIE!
Secrets of the Stars

PLYMOUTH THEATRE COMPANY at PLYMOUTH HOE THEATRE
The
Mating
Game

The sixpence went out of circulation and the Beechwood (Bowyers) factory came down. Prince Charles opened the new £60 million submarine refit complex, and the *Ark Royal* anchor was presented to the city by the Admiral of the Fleet, Lord Hill-Norton. Lord Mayor Graham Jinks accepted on behalf of the city. Westward Television's franchise was challenged by Television South-West and Westcountry Television. Ham House, after many years as a library, was refurbished as a home for the elderly. The Deer Hunter was the last film to be shown at the Odeon (the old Gaumont) in Union Street. The building re-opened in November as a Rollerina. Plymouth's swimming superstar Sharon Davies won a silver medal in the Moscow Olympics and set a new British and Commonwealth record in the 400m individual medley. There was a flurry of activity on the local music scene and a number of bands released 45's, including The Bricks, The Catholics, Smart Alec and The Mechanics. In a more substantial package of Drake 400 events, Rod Hull, Rolf Harris, Larry Grayson and Lulu were among those who appeared in a series of Sunday celebrity concerts at the Drake Film Centre. The new-style two-day (as opposed to three) Navy Days was deemed to be very successful. Argyle disposed of Chelsea in the second round of the League Cup in front of the their biggest gate of the season, 14,112.

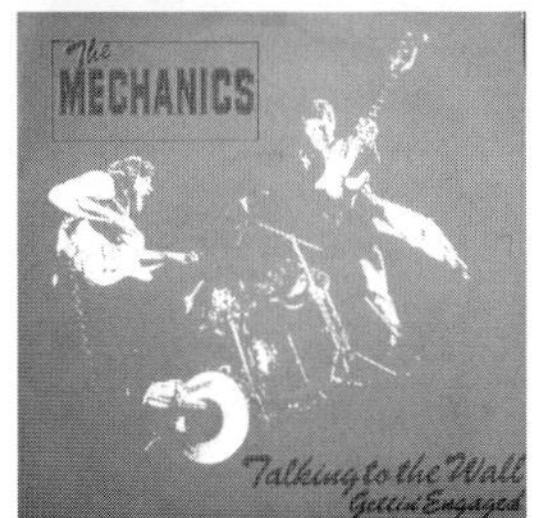
The
MECHANICS
Talking to the Wall
Gettin Engaged

THE BRICKS
beam me up Scotty warp factor two
I want to be a Startrekker just like you

This is
SCOOTER
BOYS
by SMART ALEC
Third Party, Fire and Death.

ARGYLE

IN PLYMOUTH this month...
The Empire Strikes Back
Ian Lavender
Windsurfing Regatta
PAGES
June 1980 No 2 Monthly 20p
PLYMOUTH AREA GUIDE TO ENTERTAINMENT & SPORT
Features
David Essex
Ian Calvert
The Bricks

Tune into Plymouth Sound
Holiday Fun
261
261
PLYMOUTH
SOUND
The fastest Sound
in the West
6.00a.m.'til Midnight
Local Radio at it's Best

THE HEART OF
PLYMOUTH'S
Nite
Life
Cascade
Club
CLONES
For all
bookings
'phone
PLYMOUTH
63127

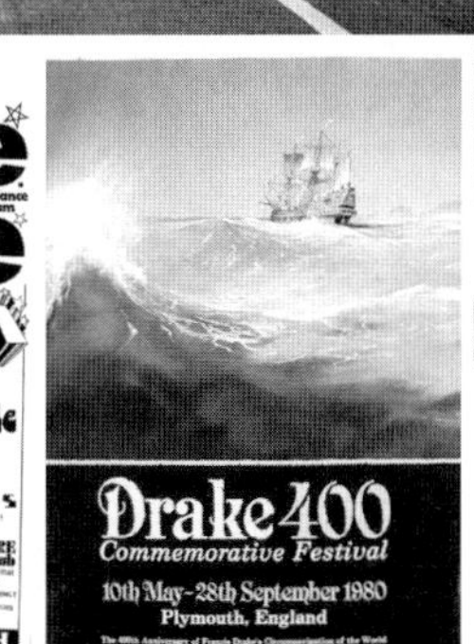
Drake 400
Commemorative Festival
10th May - 28th September 1980
Plymouth, England

Studio Theatre
Loot

HMS *Brilliant* was commissioned, Britain's last paddle-tug, RMAS *Faithful* - launched in June 1957 - was taken out of service as sirens sounded in her honour, and Devonport (Royal Albert) Hospital, was closed. In the Dockyard itself the size of the workforce had dropped to 15,000; however a local jobs bonanza was expected to follow the discovery that there was still tin and tungsten at Hemerdon Ball. The *Midweek Independent* was distributed free to 10,000 homes in Plymouth, Saltash and Torpoint each week - extra copies could be had for 6p - and the city had a new, free, listings magazine, the *Plymouth Entertainer*. British coins no longer bore the word "new" before the pence value and Prince Charles announced his engagement to 19-year-old Lady Diana Spencer. They married in July. Meanwhile 22-year-old Stella Goodier got rave reviews for her portrayal of Edith Piaf at the Hoe Theatre. Critics said it was worth coming down from London to see her performance. Former Hyde Park schoolboy Wayne Sleep brought his stunning dance show Dash! to the Palace Theatre, and Patrick Cargill starred there as Hercule Poirot in Agatha Christie's Black Coffee. Argyle's form improved - they finished seventh - and for the second season running Dave Kemp was their leading scorer. 24 times he netted in the league and he also scored in four out of their five cup games.

HOE CAFE

THE SUNDAY TIMES magazine
A special pictorial record of the day
ROYAL WEDDING

Squires

WHITBREAD THE BURTON BOYS WHITBREAD

ARGYLE
ARGYLE
ARGYLE
ARGYLE

35p
Plymouth
The Real Maritime Centre

NOT NOW DARLING
PLYMOUTH
HOE THEATRE

Plymouth was reminded of its role in the defence industry and the Dockyard was at its busiest for many years as the Battle for the Falklands got under way. Night and day the Yard bustled as men, ships and supplies were made ready. In May, news of the sinking of HMS *Sheffield* cast a gloom over the celebrations surrounding the opening of the Theatre Royal, but by the middle of June the war was all over. There was a day of rejoicing in July as thousands massed for a welcome of tears and cheers. 2,000 men rode in a coach convoy, creating the biggest traffic jam the city had ever seen. Lord Mayor Reg Scott said it could not have been a better show "if we had won the World Cup". In November Prince Andrew led a huge parade and spectacular flypast and the Crown Inn in Manor Street was renamed the General Moore, in honour of Major-General Jeremy Moore, who had accepted the Argentinian surrender on 14 June. Earlier in the year the Hoe Theatre had closed and soon demolished and in August the Palace Theatre was forced to close. Pilgrim Primary was opened and demolition began of the old school in Oxford Street. The 20p coin was introduced, boats assembled in Millbay for the Round Britain & Ireland Race, Vernon Penprase fought a British title fight with Barry McGuigan, and Ian Botham, George Best, Paul Mariner and Ian Gillan appeared at Home Park for one reason or another.

Hoe Theatre
GINGERBREAD MAN

ARGYLE
OXFORD UNITED

Theatre Royal Plymouth
TOM BAKER AS FRANK
KATE FITZGERALD AS RITA
EDUCATING RITA
Hamlet
COMEDY OF THE YEAR
RSC
8-13 November 1982 only

JESUS CHRIST SUPERSTAR
28 MAY – 12 JUNE
Theatre Royal Plymouth

Theatre Royal Plymouth
Opening season
THEATRE ROYAL PLYMOUTH

1983

The Queen visited the Royal Naval Engineering College at Manadon and the Devonort Field Gun crew swept the board at Earl's Court. The pound note was replaced by the pound coin and Theatre Royal chief Gordon Stratford quit his post after just 18 months. Twenty tons of bricks fell from the 100ft tower of Plymouth Polytechnic, St Boniface College was demolished, with vandals setting fire to it before it had been completely flattened, and Devonport Hospital was sold for redevelopment. Plans were considered for a new £1.5 million development at Queen Anne's Battery and the enquiry began into the question of the Saltash by-pass and tunnel. There was power boat racing in the Sound, the Bournemouth Sinfonietta were in the Guildhall, and BBC Radio Devon was launched at Seymour Road and from studios in Exeter, as part of the BBC's commitment to local radio. Helen Hughes, Travis Baxter, Ian Phillips, David Bassett and Douglas Mounce were among those in the opening line-up of presenters. Martin Dean was the sports producer. Fursdon Leisure Centre opened and new figures revealed that Plymouth's latest unemployment rate - 14.1% - had just leapt ahead of the national average. The area's jobless total had gone above 17,000, 1,250 of them school leavers under 18. Meanwhile the College of Further Education grew with the opening of its £1.5 m Catering Block.

Barbican Voice

The free newspaper for the Barbican and Hoe areas February 1983 No. 6

ANGER AS CITY'S PLANNERS 'SNUB' GROUP

THERE has been sharp criticism of Plymouth's Planning Committee for its refusal to meet a deputation from the Barbican Group last month.

£150 FOR FALKLAND FUND IS RAISED BY THE 'ADMIRAL'

1984

Peter Levene, adviser to Defence Secretary Michael Heseltine, recommended that private companies should take over the management of Devonport and of Rosyth Dockyard. Toshiba brought another 300 jobs to Plymouth with their £3.5 million microwave oven factory at Belliver, and it was announced that "one of the first purpose-built centres in the country for training primary school teachers" was to be established at the College of St Mark &St John at a cost of £100,000. The Armada Centre and the new Sainsbury's supermarket was opened just off the top of Armada Way and the extension to St Pancras Church, Pennycross, was blessed by the Bishop of Exeter. The Courage Brewery in Stonehouse closed and, in December, Halls Brewery in Valley Road, Plympton, brewed some "traditional best bitter". The Lockyer Tavern, near Derry's Clock, was demolished, while in Devonport work began on restoring the Guildhall, with the help of an urban aid grant of £100,000 - the largest to have been awarded outside Bristol. Drake's Island ferry was wrecked and HMS *Scylla* was back in the Dockyard. Argyle managed something few other Third Division clubs have ever done - they reached the semi-final of the FA Cup - losing 1-0 to Watford at Villa Park. Had Kevin Hodges' shot gone in, a few minutes from the final whistle, who knows what might have happened...

Pencil Sketches

PLYMOUTH
Theatre Royal
COMPANY
INSIGNIFICANCE
by Terry Johnson
The Greatest Brain of the Century
meets The Greatest Body of the Century
Thurs 10th May - Sat 2nd June
THE DRUM

Theatre Royal Plymouth
London Festival Ballet
Box Office:
Tel: (0752) 669595
12-17 March 1984
Theatre Royal Plymouth
MONDAY 30th APRIL – 5th MAY 1984
The Young Vic
THE REAL INSPECTOR HOUND
TOM STOPPARD
"AN EVENING NOT TO BE MISSED"
JEREMY JAMES TAYLOR
THE FUNNIEST DOUBLE-BILL EVER!
LAURIE ALLEN
TOM COULTHARD
TERENCE FRISBY
IAN TAYLOR
JUDY WILSON
and
SEASIDE POSTCARD
TERENCE FRISBY
'THERE'S A GIRL IN MY SOUP'
"HILARIOUS ...VERY FUNNY"

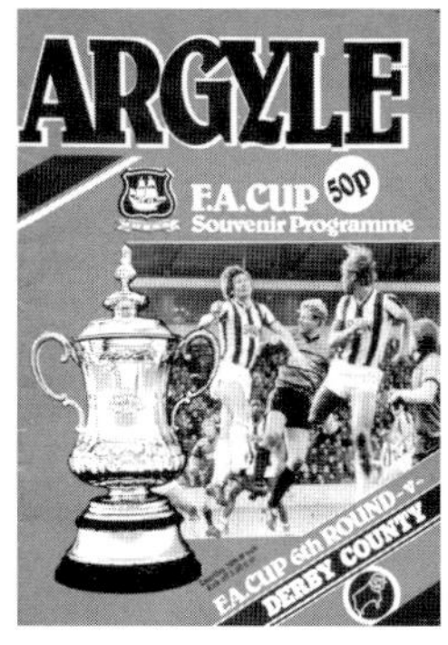
ARGYLE
F.A. CUP
50p
Souvenir Programme
F.A. CUP 6th ROUND
DERBY COUNTY

Carmenians
The Merry Widow

MATCH DAY MAGAZINE OF DERBY COUNTY
RAM
DERBY COUNTY
PLYMOUTH ARGYLE
Wednesday, March 14,
(7.30 p.m.)

OCTOBER 84
No5
BARKER
WHAT'S ON IN PLYMOUTH and the SOUTH WEST
COSTELLO IN CORNWALL
40

PLYMOUTH
ARGYLE
WATFORD
FA CUP SEMI-FINAL
14th APRIL 1984
AT VILLA PARK
BIRMINGHAM
OFFICIAL PROGRAMME

1986

Defence Secretary Michael Hesletine was in Plymouth, determined to privatise the Dockyard. "I am not getting value for money and I will get value for money." Janet Fookes took her Kerb Crawling Bill to the Commons and Sutton MP Alan Clark was in hot water over his "Bongo Bongo Land" comments. Devon firemen were increasingly reluctant to give the kiss of life in the wake of the Aids scare, and the Police Box at Home Park was moved in the course of the redevelopment of Outland Road. The Parkway was opened, the Distillery pub was established in part of the Plymouth Gin building, and the old artillery tower at Firestone Bay was converted into a restaurant. Marine Projects had grown to become Britain's biggest boat builders and there was a new Pilgrim Fathers' board put up on the side of Island House listing all the male and female Pilgrims. St Joseph's Church in Devonport began holding services, and British Rail were hoping to get approval for plans to put superstores on the old Friary Station site. Brittany Ferries were offering Ferry And Drive Freedom weekends in France for £25 per person, preliminary work was under way on the Saltash Tunnel, and the Torpoint ferry, *Lynher,* was lengthened by 50 feet. Argyle were knocked out of the FA Cup by Hereford, while in the league Tommy Tynan scored 31 goals - more than the rest of the team put together!

PLYMOUTH
STAR
INCORPORATING THE MidWeek INDEPENDENT
PLYMOUTH
Devon's
SEASIDE
CITY!
KANE
38 LOOE STREET
PLYMOUTH ARTS CENTRE
TEL: 660060
SEPTEMBER
OCTOBER
1985
Sound/Vision Exhibition..... Cinema..... Music.....
Workshops..... Restaurant..... Darkroom
PLYMOUTH MARATHON
SUNDAY JUNE 2 1985
INSIDE
Tokina LENSES
£85.95
THREE-YEAR GUARANTEE
Evening Herald
Citizens' Guide '85
Issued with the Western Evening Herald
ARGYLE
The Pilgrims
P.A.F.C.
NEWPORT COUNTY
match magazine

1988

Plymouth's visitor capacity increased with the opening of the Copthorne Hotel off North Cross roundabout. The Roundabout pub at Marsh Mills was pulled down to make way for redevelopment, and the fountain at St Andrew's Cross roundabout was turned on for the first time. Queen Anne's Battery Marina came into use and Plymouth was the host for the two-handed transatlantic race. 12,000 Devonport Dockyard workers walked out in protest over the proposed privatisation of the yard and pupils walked out of Stoke Damerel High School for the last time as another of Plymouth's older educational establishments closed. Sutton High School had earlier moved in with them following the closure of their Regent Street premises. Boots bought out Farley's Plymouth operation and the firm's Kendal plant for a knock-down £18 million. There was talk of redundancies. Plymouth's busmen were in striking form and there were problems on the roads when snow brought much of the city to a slippery standstill. Mercedes, the Mechanics, Porrij and the Blue Cadillacs were among the bands to play a charity concert at the Academy for the local Leukaemia appeal, while closure of Greenbank and Freedom Fields loomed as plans for 1,200 beds at Derriford moved closer to fruition. Dave Smith's Argyle won 13 of their last 15 games (Tynan scored 10 goals in the last 9 games) and were promoted.

Western Evening Herald

No. 31,248 17p

PLYMOUTH, SATURDAY, MARCH 29, 1986

Plymouth Presents
CROMWELL
GLOBE THEATRE
Wed 17 - Sat 20 Dec. at 7.30
tickets £2 from Chapter & Verse, Virgin

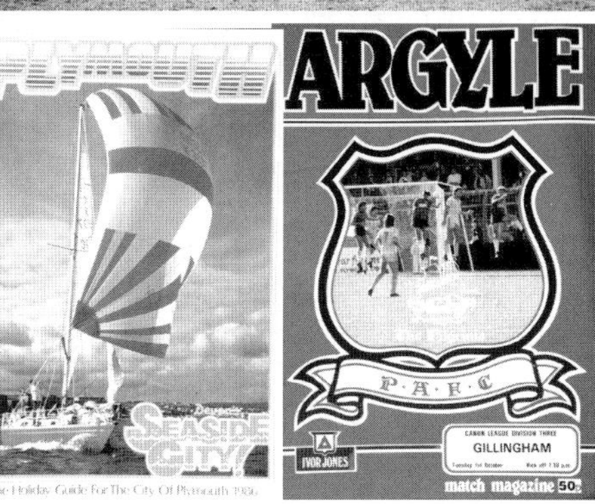

1987

Pedestrianisation of the City Centre got under way and work began on the new car park and Homebase building off Western Approach. The Government leased Devonport Dockyard and its facilities to Devonport Management Limited (DML) who lost little time in shedding 3,000 jobs. Devonport-based frigate HMS *Broadsword* went into the Yard for a major nine-month refit after its return from two months' service in the Gulf with the Armilla Patrol. It was announced that electronics giant Texas Instruments were to close their Plymouth factory with the loss of 320 jobs and South West Water workers were told to gear up for privatisation. In August, Chase Webb opened a new £15 million factory after a huge blaze had destroyed their old premises, killing three employees. The Submarine (formerly the Camel's Head) pub closed to make way for a new road and after years of neglect and a couple of failed attempts, Boringdon Hall was restored by Peter Malkin. The SDP took eight seats on the City Council, the Liberals took two, and former Plymouth College boy Richard Deacon won the Turner Prize for art. Musicals old and new were staged at the Theatre Royal with Andrew Lloyd Webber's *Evita* and Gilbert & Sullivan's *Pirates Of Penzance*. Plymouth Argyle, back in the Second Division again, finished a creditable seventh, despite winning only one of their last eight games.

BRYMON
G-BARB
HJY 1
DAVID OWEN
RODGERS & HAMMERSTEIN'S
SOUTH PACIFIC
Plymouth Albion R.F.C
Beacon Park Plymouth
Official Programme
THE BAND OF HER MAJESTY'S ROYAL MARINES
FLAG OFFICER PLYMOUTH
1987 ROYAL TOURNAMENT
DEVONPORT
FIELD GUN CREW
PLYMOUTH
ARGYLE
CENTENARY YEAR
DIVISION TWO 1986/87

1988

The Queen inspected the new Sundial in the city centre and became the first official visitor to the Plymouth Dome, even though the attraction wasn't yet open. Her Majesty also unveiled the commemorative plaque marking the 400th anniversary of the Armada and was guest of honour at an Armada Night Dinner. Plymouth-born composer Ron Goodwin conducted the Band of the Royal Marines. The Queen's Hotel, the United Service and other parts of Edgcumbe Street (Union Street) were demolished and Widey Technical School was closed as plans were drawn up to redevelop the site for housing. The last cargo of coal was delivered to Bayly's Wharf, in Sutton Harbour, and BBC Radio Devon moved into the old Treasury building in Catherine Street. The pound note ceased to be legal tender and anti-fur activists claimed responsibility for the Dingles fire-bomb. The Academy, Rockafella's and Oscars were the latest names, although not necessarily the latest venues, in Plymouth's clubland, and after a noble attempt to keep HMS *Plymouth* (aboard which the Argentinian surrender had been accepted, marking the end of the Falklands War) as a visitor attraction, the famous ship left port. The Armada Experience opened in New Street, on the Barbican, and 7,000 people walked through the new road tunnel a week before the £13 million Saltash by-pass officially opened.

AN EXTRAORDINARY
JOURNEY THROUGH TIME

PLYMOUTH DOME

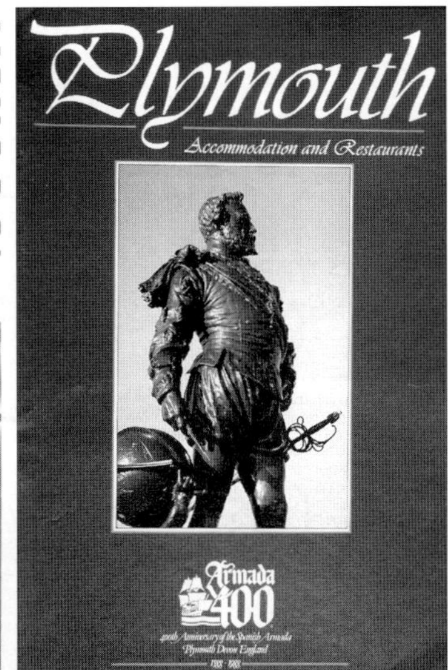

HMS *Drake* celebrated its centenary and Dingles reopened after a major refurbishment, three months after the fire. The Dome was officially opened on The Hoe, and RAF Mountbatten began preparing for closure. The Royal Western Yacht Club moved from its base in West Hoe to purpose-built premises at Queen Anne's Battery and the seventeenth-century warehouse on the eastern side of Sutton Pool, one of the few in the country still with water on three sides, was converted into a pub, The China House. Princess Anne visited HMS *Amazon* and Saltram House. IRA threats sparked unprecedented security measures: pubs were emptied of servicemen, streets were cleared and parked cars and shorelines were searched. Marine Projects, with 1,150 employees, were reckoned to be the third largest boat builders in Europe. Meanwhile work began in Devonport Dockyard on a fleet of eleven steel yachts that DML were building for the British Steel Challenge - the Round-the-World Race that interntaional yachtsman Chay Blyth was organising. The submarine *Opportune* completed its refit - it was the 28th Oberon and Porpoise Class sub to be refitted in the Yard. Defence chiefs revealed plans to release 30 acres of building land at Seaton Barracks next to the expanding Derriford Business Park, and there were elephants and other wild animals at Gandey's Circus in Central Park.

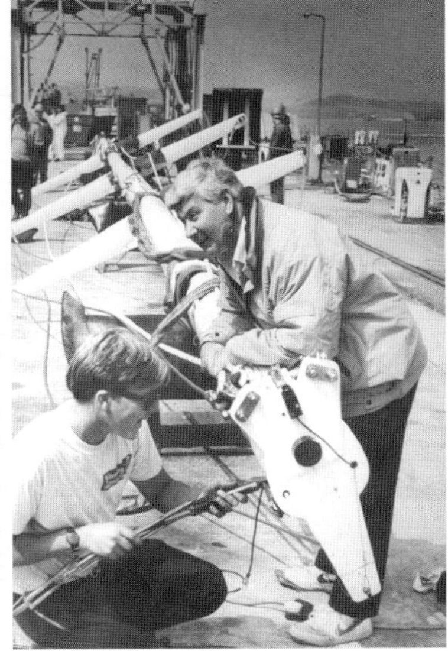

ADMIRALS
73
80

ADMIRALS

BOAT SHOW

The Armada Experience

RICHARD·DEACON
new sculpture
Sat 11th Nov–Sat 23rd Dec 1989

Plymouth
1989

Plymouth
ARGYLE

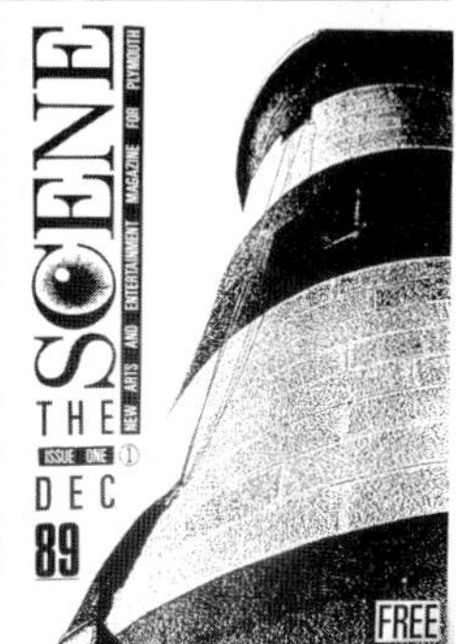
THE SCENE
NEW ARTS AND ENTERTAINMENT MAGAZINE FOR PLYMOUTH
ISSUE ONE
DEC
89
FREE

1990

Winds of more than 110 mph cut a trail of devastation across the area. Two hundred dockyard buildings were damaged, as were thousands of private houses. The demolition contract was awarded for Prince Rock Power Station, and work on Marsh Mills Roundabout was under way. Ranco Controls won a £6 million order from Germany's leading refrigerator manufacturer, and the Co-operative warehouse, rebuilt on North Quay in 1960, was demolished to make way for new flats. Prior to the installation of lock gates across Sutton Pool, tests were carried out on West Pier. Almost £1 million would be spent filling the cracks and fissures found. The number of apprentices starting work in the Yard was slashed to 75, as the Royal Navy opened its new Camel's Head Creek base. DML won its first Royal Fleet Auxiliary refit - on the *Grey Rover*. Sutton MP Alan Clark asked for a quick release of the Royal William Yard; locally and nationally the Poll Tax proved to be unpopular, and Mrs Thatcher resigned in November. *My Fair Lady* was at the Theatre Royal, and there were strippers every Wednesday at Zena's. Stores planning to open on Sundays were warned by Plymouth City Council that they could have their executives jailed, and Richard Deacon's "Moor" was put up on part of the old railway viaduct in Victoria Park. Argyle signed Keith Edwards in a bid to end their recent goal famine.

Farley Health Products

Farley's
Rusks

MILK RACE
STAGE
WINNER
MILK RACE

CUTTY SARK
TALL SHIPS' RACE
Plymouth
4-7 July 1990
Plymouth
Set a course for 1990

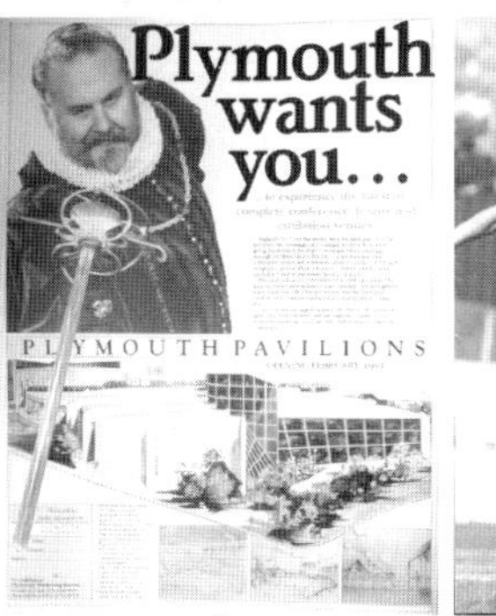
Plymouth
wants
you...
PLYMOUTH PAVILIONS

ARGYLE
v
OXFORD

GRAHAM LITTLE
TESTIMONIAL

Prince Charles and Lady Diana visited Devonport Dockyard, meeting staff involved in preparing ships for the war zone in the Gulf. In July, HMS *Brave*, then the longest-serving Gulf War ship, returned to a hero's welcome. Later in the year there were more than 20 ships on show at Navy Days including the very latest Type-23 frigate HMS *Marlborough*. Prime Minister John Major visited Plymouth Dome, and the city's latest attraction - Plymouth Pavillions - was opened, with its kidney-shaped skating rink and flume-fed leisure pool. Plymouth City Airport celebrated its 60th birthday, Brittany Ferries announced that they had carried 142,620 passengers on their Roscoff route, and a further 51,695 on the Santander crossing. A Park & Ride scheme was introduced from Home Park to the city centre and Dame Janet Fookes and Lord Mayor Betty Easton officiated at the opening of the Burleigh Manor estate (on the site of the erstwhile Burleigh School, and, before that, Burleigh House). Plans were announced to close the Royal Naval Hospital at Stonehouse by March 1993. Ritzy was named the South West disco of the year, the *Rocky Horror Show* was at the Theatre Royal, and there was a local petrol price war with 4-star dropping to 226.8p per gallon. In the local government elections, the Labour Party took control of the city council with 41 seats. The Conservatives won 19.

THE TOMMY TYNAN BENEFIT GAME

PLYMOUTH ARGYLE v ASTON VILLA

WEDNESDAY 7th AUGUST 1991 KICK OFF 7.30pm

Plymouth

1991

Where Devon meets Cornwall

The Polytechnic of the South West became Plymouth University with a staff of around 1,000 and some 8,500 students. RAF Mountbatten closed and Devonort Dockyard's roll call dropped below 5,000. Work on the £100 million refit of the Fleet nuclear submarine HMS *Trafalgar* got under way, and the new £24.9 million Marsh Mills flyover was launched. The number of beds at Derriford Hospital rose to 650. Gary Streeter was the new MP for Sutton and David Jamieson won Devonport back for Labour. Later in the year Jamieson and workers from the Dockyard handed a petition into Downing Street: "Give Us Trident". Under the Government's "right to buy", more than 7,000 council homes had been sold. The council stock of houses was still nearly 20,000 but only 48 new council houses were built this year. The Queen visited the Royal William Yard as the Navy began its withdrawal - stage one of a £45 million land deal. The £27 million facelift of the Royal Citadel was completed. A coffer dam was created across Coxside Creek, councillors gave the go-ahead for two new supermarkets at Marsh Mills, and Brittany Ferries said they were going to switch their biggest ferry, the 31,000 ton *Val de Loire*, to Plymouth, doubling its service to Roscoff. Plymouth Argyle, relegated from Division Two, found themselves in the new Second Division following the League's restructuring.

michael ball
one step out of time

Brittany Ferries

Western Morning News

Turbosound

PLYMOUTH CITYBUS
1892
1992
CENTENARY
ONE HUNDRED YEARS OF SERVICE
A Commemorative Review in Words and Pictures

PLYMOUTH
ARGYLE
FOOTBALL CLUB
v LEICESTER CITY
Saturday 11th January 1992. Kick-Off 3.00p.m.
Official Sponsor Sunday Independent
Todays Match Sponsor, Whitbread Beer Company
Barclays League Division Two • Official Programme £1

FREE
SCENE
MUSIC/ARTS MAGAZINE
BATMAN
ALTERNATIVE COMEDY
THEATRE
CLUBS & MORE
THE FAMILY CAT INTERVIEW
THE MONTHLY ENTERTAINMENT GUIDE FOR PLYMOUTH

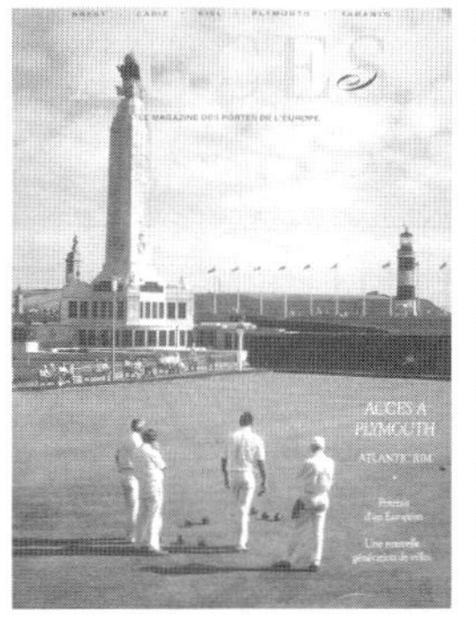
ACCES A PLYMOUTH

1842
Walter C. Parson
1992

The *Western Evening Herald* and *Western Morning News* newspapers moved their offices out to an impressive new ship-shape building, designed by Nicholas Grimshaw, at Derriford. Improvements costing £160,000 were carried out at Derriford Roundabout, just three months after the completion of the £1 million dual-carriageway scheme between Belliver and Woolwell. Unhappy with legislation limiting fishing time, protestors barricaded themselves in at the MAFF (Ministry of Agriculture and Food) Offices on the Barbican. Meanwhile protesters unhappy with the decision to close Tinside Pool were denied permission to organise a petition in Plymouth City Centre. Alison Stone became the city's new Chief Executive, succeeding Mike Boxall. In June, Defence Secretary Malcolm Rifkind announces in the Commons that Devonport has been selected to refit Britain's Trident nuclear submarine fleet. In a terrible tragedy off Lyme Bay, four Southway School pupils are drowned during a canoe trip. Oscar Wilde's *Ideal Husband* is performed at the Theatre Royal. Plymouth University adopted a Continental and American-style semester structure for the new academic year, and England goalkeeping legend Peter Shilton appeared a number of times for Argyle in his role as Player-Manager. The team finished mid-table with average gates of 6,211 - up 14.5 per cent on the previous season.

DEVONPOR NEEDS TRIDENT
WE WON'T.. LET DEVONPORT BLEED TO DEATH!
GIVE US TRIDENT GIVE US A FUTURE!

PLYMOUTH
A NEW HISTORY

Herald
ONE BIG SHOUT FOR THE YARD!
Herald
Their future in your hands, Mr Major
Herald
IT MUST BE DEVONPORT
Herald
DEVONPORT EXPECTS . . .
Herald
VICTORY!
FIRST WORLD
QUALITY CLOTHING FROM AROUND THE WORLD
MORE STOCK TO COME
10 DRAKE CIRCUS, PLYMOUTH DEVON
SPECIAL SUMMER BARGAINS!!
ROCK AT THE BREAKWATER
JULY
PLYMOUTHS ORIGINAL VENUE BAR
The BREAKWATER Tel 664556

PLYMOUTH ARGYLE
BARCLAYS LEAGUE DIVISION TWO • OFFICIAL PROGRAMME £1.20
v FULHAM
MATCHDAY SPONSOR

We are on the move
Herald
Head office is:
17 Brest Road,
Derriford Business park,
Plymouth PL6 5AA.
Tel: (0752) 765500
Our CLASSIFIED SHOP has moved just around the corner
to
107, ARMADA WAY
(Next to British Gas)
PLYMOUTH
Classified Advertising (0752) 770770

SCENE
MUSIC • ARTS MAGAZINE
SUMMER FESTIVALS
PLUS BENJAMIN ZEPHANIAH
MANIC STREET PREACHERS INTERVIEW
FREE

ADRIAN BURROWS
TESTIMONIAL
PLYMOUTH ARGYLE
v
SHEFFIELD WEDNESDAY
WED 21st JULY 1993
KICK-OFF 7.30PM.
TODAYS MATCH SPONSOR
FRANK ELFORD SPORTS

1994

After only three months, Tesco ordered contractors to stop work on the £35 million supermarket project at Marsh Mills, meanwhile work continued on the Sainsbury's site on the other side of the roundabout. The lock gates across the mouth of Sutton Pool came into use, and entertainer Roy Castle finished his 1,200-mile Tour Of Hope on Plymouth Hoe. He'd raised £1 million in a week. Plymouth claimed victory in its 20-year battle for independence after the Local Government Commission backed the city's "Home Rule" demands. Too little surface ship work prompted more jobs cuts in the Dockyard. DML Managing Director Mike Leece said that implementing 8,000 job cuts in seven years had been difficult and upsetting. The workforce was now 3,500. The problems had been worsened by the departure of HMS *Illustrious*, the Royal Navy's most advanced warship. DML won the contract to refit the ten yachts that had taken part in the 1992 Challenge race and they already had the contract to build another five for the 1996 race. In August, Central Park played host to the Heineken Music Festival. Tom Robinson, Toyah, Jools Holland, The Stranglers and Desmond Dekker were among the headliners. Reach, The Retreat, Watershed, Sha Gov and Daddy Teacha were among the local acts. A couple of home defeats near the end of the season saw Argyle just miss out on promotion.

SAVE THE
SOUTHWEST
DEFENCE
INDUSTRY

Pavilions
WHATS on
SPRING CALENDAR
APRIL
MAY
JUNE 94

Plymouth Citybus
Annual Report & Accounts
1993/94

SAINSBURY'S
Opens here Autumn 1994.
Birse

TWO-HANDED
TRANSATLANTIC RACE
SOUVENIR MAGAZINE 1994
JEWELS IN PLYMOUTH'S
CROWN
RACE BRIEFING
THE CORINTHIAN SPIRIT
THE MEN, THE WOMEN,
AND THEIR SAILING
MACHINES
Organised in conjunction with The Royal Western Yacht Club of England
£1/$2

THE
WARREN FAMILY
ARGYLE
v
BURNLEY
Lucozade
SPORT
WEDNESDAY 18TH
MAY 1994
KICK-OFF 7.45 p.m.
OFFICIAL SPONSOR
Thompsons

A38

B29
B7

PLYMOUTH • AUGUST 1994
SCENE
Special festival
issue!
Free

The
Acoustic
Cafe
At The
Breakwater
Monday's
8.30pm - 1am

D-DAY 50
PLYMOUTH
1944

RIVAL
RECORDS,TAPES,CDs & VIDEO
ROCK, POP, METAL, INDIE,
DANCE, BLUES.
GOOD QUALITY SECOND HAND
CDs BOUGHT AND SOLD
DOWNSTAIRS
WE HAVE A MASSIVE RANGE OF
T-SHIRTS, SWEATSHIRTS, CAPS, POSTERS,
POSTCARDS & ROCK MERCHANDISE.
CONCERT TICKETS
SOLE
BOOKING AGENTS
FOR
CONCERT TRAVEL
+ ALL LOCAL
TICKETS
CHECK US OUT!
64 ROYAL PARADE • PLYMOUTH • 221952

whatson
MAY - AUGUST 1994
BARBICAN THEATRE
CASTLE STREET · PLYMOUTH · PL1 2NJ

1995

The fish market moved to a new £3 million building, designed by the Architects Design Group, on reclaimed land at Coxside. Barbican-based artist Robert Lenkiewicz had a major exhibition outside the city - in Birmingham - and sold hundreds of thousands of pounds worth of work. The "biggest party in fifty years" was staged on The Hoe to celebrate the 50th Anniversary of VE Day. The second Keyham Carnival and Fun Day was proclaimed a great success and nearly every street in Keyham entered a float. Argyle Chairman Dan McCauley announced that Peter Shilton had been suspended. It was to be too late for the Pilgrims though as Argyle, who never managed to get above mid-table all season, were relegated to the Third Division (the old Fourth Division) for the first time in the club's history. The Plymouth Half Marathon, revived the previous year by DML Sports & Social Club, attracted over 1,000 runners and thousands more lined the course to cheer the competitors. DML meanwhile won a £20 million heat management contract to design, procure and install new chilled water systems into Trafalgar Class nuclear submarines. Antiques dealer Mike Antonucci was one of two big winners locally on the National Lottery - he won £2.8 million. Saltram House was host to the stars as Hugh Grant, Kate Winslet and Emma Thompson were here for the filming of *Sense & Sensibility.*

ADMIRALS

BRITISH OP

SCENE
Sept '95
local bands make a stand!
plus
FREE
toby jepson, joan armatrading, heavy stereo
full listings and more!

Streets of the South West '95
OF STREET THEATRE

LORD MAYOR'S DAY
Saturday 20th May 1995
Glorious Plymouth
Silver Jubilee
1970 - 1995
Organised by Port of Plymouth
Junior Chamber of Commerce
OFFICIAL PROGRAMME 50p

Beryl Cook
A Twentieth Anniversary Exhibition
Saturday 11 November - Saturday 23 December
PLYMOUTH ARTS CENTRE

CROWNHILL FORT
EVENT
WEEKEND
1st-2nd July 1995
PROGRAMME
OF
EVENTS
Crownhill Fort, Crownhill Fort Road,
Plymouth, PL6 5BY.
Telephone & fax: (01752) 793754

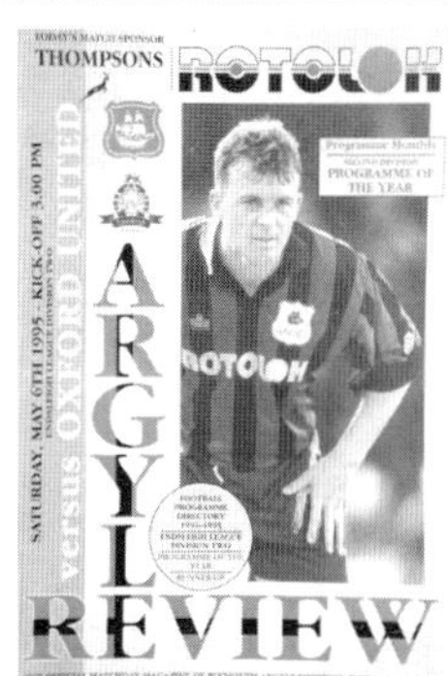
THOMPSONS
ROTOLOK
SATURDAY, MAY 6TH 1995 · KICK-OFF 3.00 PM
versus OXFORD UNITED
ARGYLE
REVIEW

1996

Coxside Creek between Lockyer's Quay and Johnson's Quay - which had been used to construct the new lock gates - was infilled and Whitbread built a new pub on the site. North Quay House was completed on North Quay. Sutton Harbour Company and English Partnerships moved in. Plymouth beat off competition from 13 other UK cities to get the prize of ten full Royal Shakespeare productions in the Theatre Royal and the Drum. Former Plymouth College pupil Pete Goss effected the heroic rescue of Frenchman Raphael Dinelli in the Vendee Globe Round-the-World Race, off the coast of Tasmania. Devonport Yachts, the specialist yacht group at DML, was awarded the contract by Chay Blyth's Challenge Business Limited to build 11 steel-hulled yachts for a new round-the-world race in 2000. They also agreed seven new contracts - five on warships, two on coastal vessels - that amounted to £70 million worth of business to the Yard. Local folk-rockers The Retreat signed a national recording deal and lottery winner Mike Antonucci released a single with one of Plymouth's finest guitarists, Phil Lean. Calling themselves Happy Daze, the song title, inspired by the lottery slogan, was It Could Be You. Argyle meanwhile, under Neil Warnock, heaved themselves out of the national league basement at the first attempt - via the play-offs. Some 30,000 fans made the trip to Wembley.

Ancient Waters

ROADSIDE
Mrs Jones
IT COULD BE YOU
HAPPY DAZE

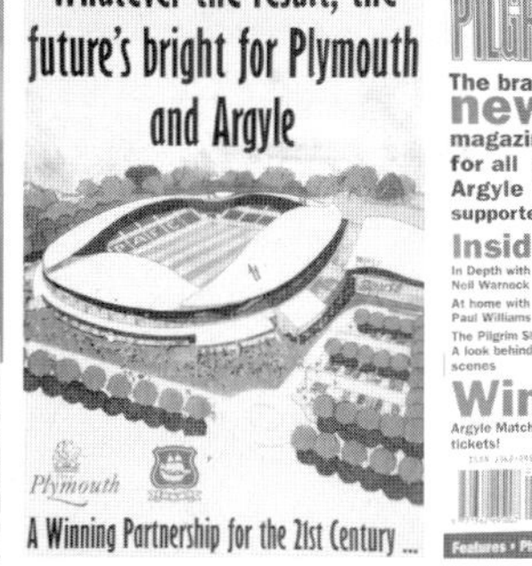

Whatever the result, the future's bright for Plymouth and Argyle
Plymouth
A Winning Partnership for the 21st Century

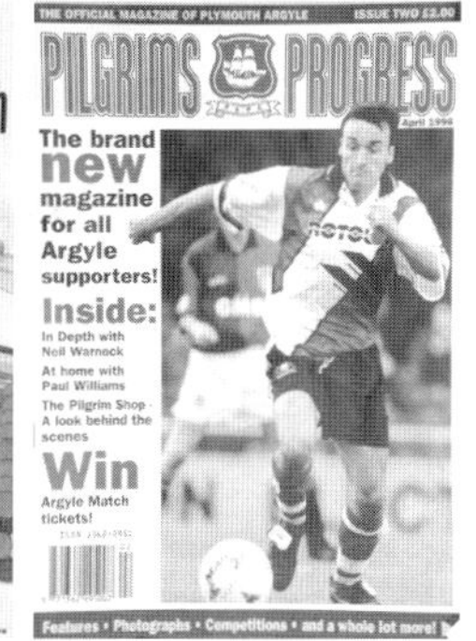

THE OFFICIAL MAGAZINE OF PLYMOUTH ARGYLE
PILGRIMS PROGRESS
The brand new magazine for all Argyle supporters!
Inside:
In Depth with Neil Warnock
At home with Paul Williams
The Pilgrim Shop A look behind the scenes
Win Argyle Match tickets!
Features • Photographs • Competitions • and a whole lot more!

Endsleigh
INSURANCE LEAGUE
DIVISION THREE
PLAY OFF FINAL

1997

Tavistock snooker star Andy Hick lost in the British Open to Nigel Bond in the Pavilions in April but won the Benson & Hedges Championhip at St Mellion in November. The Pavilions also proved to be a successful sporting venue for Plymouth Raiders basketball team. Meanwhile among the pop acts to visit the venue this year were Cast, Suede, Prodigy, the Manic Street Preachers and Jamiroquai. Lottery chiefs gave the thumbs-up to a £3.2 million water sports centre at Mountbatten, and plans were revealed for a £9 million leisure development at Coxside. A replica of Captain Cook's *Endeavour* visited Sutton Harbour, Cook sailed from Plymouth on each of his famous voyages to the Southern Hemisphere. Plymouth Arts Centre got a £60,000 lease of life from South West Arts. The Soundwaves festival on the Hoe was a spectacular success. Bob Geldof and Bonnie Tyler headlined, but among the other acts, Teignmouth band Muse were the ones with the brightest future. On Mutley Plain, the former Lexterten furniture store was transformed into the Hogshead, as the big breweries started chasing the growing student market. Dartington Glass moved into the transformed former fishmarket, and Argyle struggled on their return to the Second Division and crashed out of the FA Cup to Peterborough after promising wins against against Fulham (5-0) and Exeter City (4-1) in the early rounds.

THE MARITIME
GALLERY
BARBICAN GALLERY
BRITISH
OPEN '97
PLYMOUTH ARGYLE F.C
MAIN ENTRANCE TURNSTILES
rootjoose
Can't Keep Living This Way
ARGYLE REVIEW
Saturday 3rd May 1997
AFC Bournemouth
Discover the Attractions of Plymouth.
Plymouth
Hesitation Blues

1998

The impressive National Marine Aquarium opens alongside the Fishmarket at Coxside. Designed by Lacey, Hickey & Caley it almost instantly became Plymouth's premier visitor attraction. Another major crowd-puller was the National Firework Competition which was viewed from The Hoe. Tens of thousands "oohed and aahed" together. The Hoe also played host to the annual visit of the Radio 1 Roadshow and the city's Soundwaves spectacular, with Leo Sayer, Republica, Big Country and locally-managed Electrasy. The erstwhile Gaumont Cinema in Union Street had its biggest refurbishment to date and was relaunched as a series of interlinked clubs - The Millennium Complex. Further down the street the Jaeger clothing factory closed, while in the other direction the Significant Half bar-restaurant opened in the restyled Co-operative building, henceforth known as Derrys. On Mutley Plain two new licensed premises were created - Boomerangs Sports Bar and Bar Italia. The £154 million, Devonport-based HMS *Ocean* was commissioned. The Glasgow-built carrier was built to carry 500 troops (plus a further 300 in emergencies). Turnbulls, Britain's first self-service garage, closed, while Newnham hosted races for cars, bikes, motorbikes and horse-drawn carriages. And for the second time in recent years Argyle found themselves floundering at the foot of Division Two.

TURNBULLS
PLYMOUTH
RAIDERS
soccer
exclusive interviews with the west's premier stars
park life
ARENA
Row: KK
TIERED
Seat: 28
THE PILGRIMS
ARGYLE REVIEW
MUSE

1999

Plymouth was the biggest city in Britain to experience the totality of the Eclipse. Many thousands gathered on The Hoe to witness the event. Few knew quite what to expect - the darkness was truly eerie and the huge crowd broke into spontaneous applause when the sun broke through again. The Prince Regent, in Union Street, restyled itself the Eclipse and the Millbridge at Stoke became the Millenniumbridge as people geared themselves up for the party of a lifetime. Schools, colleges and communities prepared millennial projects and the city geared up for another spectacular on The Hoe. More pubs opened in student areas, most notably the three-storey Roundabout/It's A Scream below the Library in the old Britannic Assurance Building. In town, another Hogshead opened, this time in the ground floor of what had been Pophams. At Coxside, Caprice, one of the world's most famous blondes, and film buff Jonathan Ross, launched the £15 million Warner Village Complex - a 15-screen multiplex, the biggest in the South West - with attendant bars, night club, bowling alley and restaurants. Tavistock-based Equation enjoyed a hugely successful tour of America, Muse released their debut album Showbiz and played an acoustic set in Plymouth's HMV. All Saints and Stereophonics played the Pavilions and Argyle played out a fairly uneventful season in Division Three, Marshall topscoring.

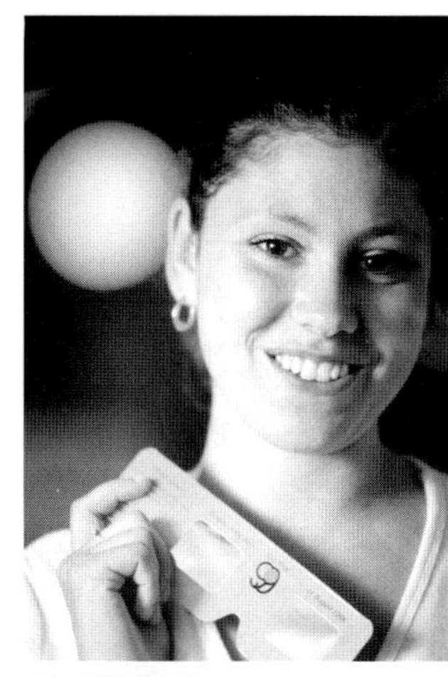

welcome

this is
THE TOTAL
£1
eclipse
GUIDE
Light show
Herald

Plymouth
Citybus
Timetable
SuperRider
• All The Buses • All The Times • All The Routes

The Bus Station Loonies
LOONIES
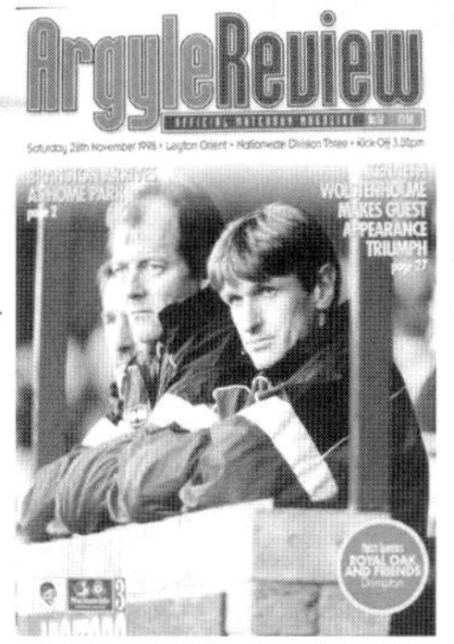
ArgyleReview

delaware
eleven eleven
11:11
Getting Closer

The Midnight countdown was moments out and fireworks were missed in the mist, but the people partied on. The new Millennium was celebrated in style and then it was very much business as usual. The Drake Cinema closed, leaving Union Street without a picture house for the first time since moving pictures came to Plymouth over a hundred years earlier. At the other end of the block the former Grevan BMW car showroom closed and was reopened as the Union Rooms - Wetherspoons' second Plymouth venture. Union Street itself was the subject of a major community production at the Theatre Royal. Hundreds of local amateurs and first-time actors appeared, echoing the success of the earlier High Heels In The Rubble. The Mountbatten Centre opened on the rapidly-redeveloping Mount Batten headland, and the Barbican Jazz Cafe opened in the former Quay Wine Bar (it had also been known as Dirty Dick's, Admiral Jasper's and the Matilda Cafe in recent years). Plymouth tribute band the Fab Beatles appeared in the prime-time TV show Battle Of The Fantasy Bands. Paul Macgregor, plucked from non-league obscurity, helped to steer Argyle close to the play-off zone, but the side remained in the Third Division. Devon made the final of the Tetley Bitter County Championship with half of Plymouth Albion's team in the squad. Dr Doolittle with Philip Scofield visits the Theatre Royal.

2000

REGENT
UNION ST PLYMOUTH
Welcome to Paradise
An exhibition about Union Street as part of the Theatre Royal's Union Street Project
At the Theatre Royal, Royal Parade
Admission Free

DEBENHAMS
DEBENHAMS

ELEVATOR SUITE
MAN IN A TOWEL

AM · FM
PLYMOUTH SOUND
RADIO

97 FM
11 52 AM

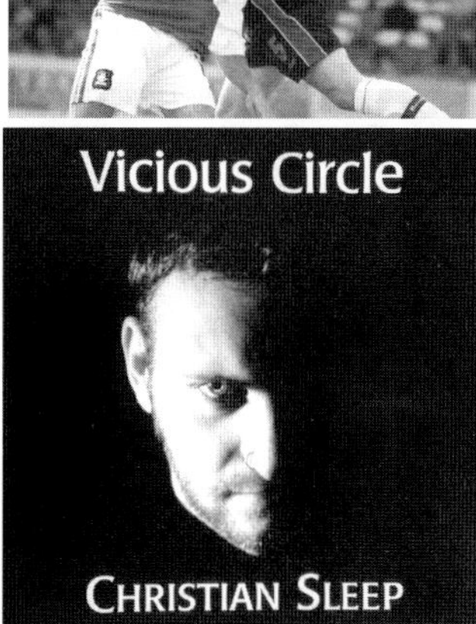

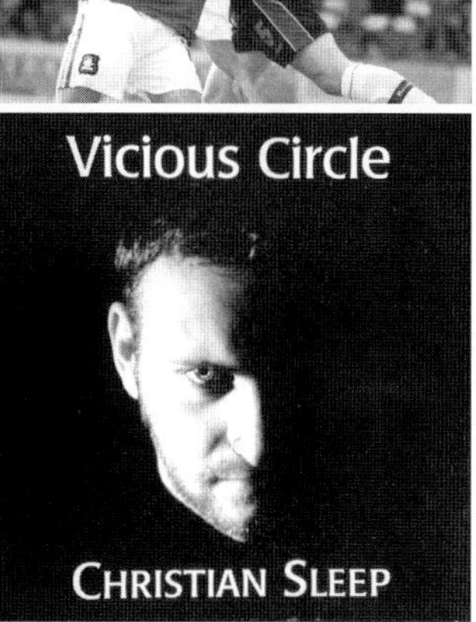
Vicious Circle
CHRISTIAN SLEEP

VINCE LEE
BIG COMBO

TWICKENHAM
THE HOME OF ENGLAND RUGBY
TETLEY'S BITTER COUNTY CHAMPIONSHIP CENTENARY FINALS DAY
ENTER BY GATES H & J
NORTH LOWER

Plymouth
GLADIATOR
Showing At 20:40
Fri 28.7.00
VILLAGE
Screen 4
Section Main

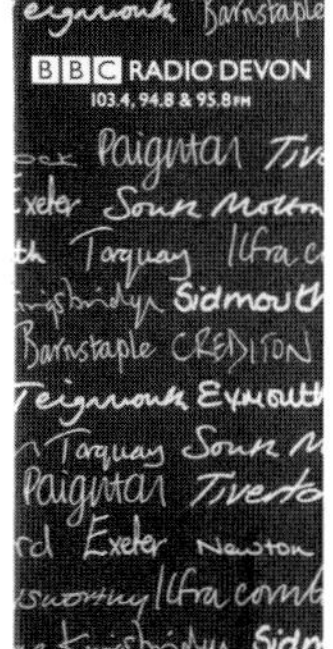
Teignmouth Barnstaple
BBC RADIO DEVON
103.4, 94.8 & 95.8FM
Paignton
Exeter
Torquay Ilfracombe
Kingsbridge Sidmouth
Barnstaple CREDITON
Teignmouth Exmouth
Torquay
Paignton Tiverton
Exeter Newton
Kingsbridge

DISCOVER PLYMOUTH
with
GUIDE FRIDAY
& Citybus

Joey the Lips
LIVE!

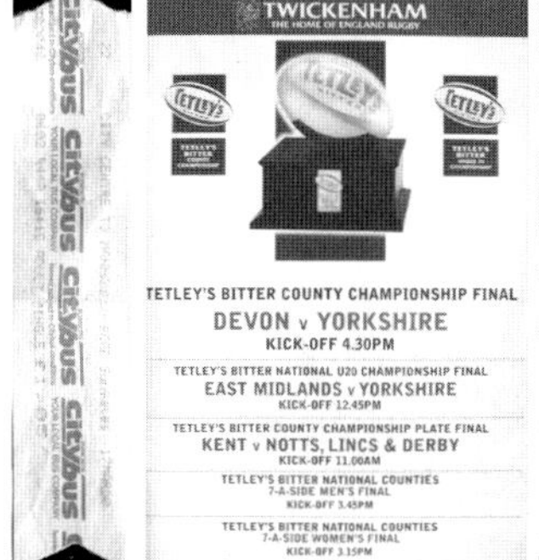
citybus
TWICKENHAM
THE HOME OF ENGLAND RUGBY
TETLEY'S BITTER COUNTY CHAMPIONSHIP FINAL
DEVON v YORKSHIRE
KICK-OFF 4.30PM
TETLEY'S BITTER NATIONAL U20 CHAMPIONSHIP FINAL
EAST MIDLANDS v YORKSHIRE
KICK-OFF 12.45PM
TETLEY'S BITTER COUNTY CHAMPIONSHIP PLATE FINAL
KENT v NOTTS, LINCS & DERBY
KICK-OFF 11.00AM
TETLEY'S BITTER NATIONAL COUNTIES
7-A-SIDE MEN'S FINAL
KICK-OFF 3.45PM
TETLEY'S BITTER NATIONAL COUNTIES
7-A-SIDE WOMEN'S FINAL
KICK-OFF 3.15PM

2001

Former England international Graham Dawe is the man who made the difference for Plymouth Albion as the side went through the season winning every game, easily taking the league title. Plymouth Raiders also had a good season but the only ray of hope for Argyle came late as the appointment of former Scottish international Paul Sturrock promised better things for the coming season rather than the current one. Pete Goss's revolutionary designed *Team Phillips* is heartbreakingly abandoned in violent storms. The Royal Navy's Gunnery School, HMS *Cambridge*, closed at Wembury and telecommunications giant JDS Uniphase close their Plymouth base as the global recession hits them. Yet more buildings were converted as pubs around the Plymouth University campus, including Jack Cham's in Ebrington Street and the Skiving Skolar just up from the Museum & Art Gallery. Local band Muse, who last played to 200 at Tramps, Bretonside, played to a full house at the Pavilions; the Buffseeds were signed to a national label straight after coming off stage at the Cooperage, and Plymouth's Bus Station Loonies set up a certified Guinness World Record by playing 25 gigs in 25 different venues around the city in just 12 hours. Faith Brown starred in the first UK touring version of Andrew Lloyd Webber's *Sunset Boulevard*, and his *Whistle Down The Wind* was also staged here.

bex marshall

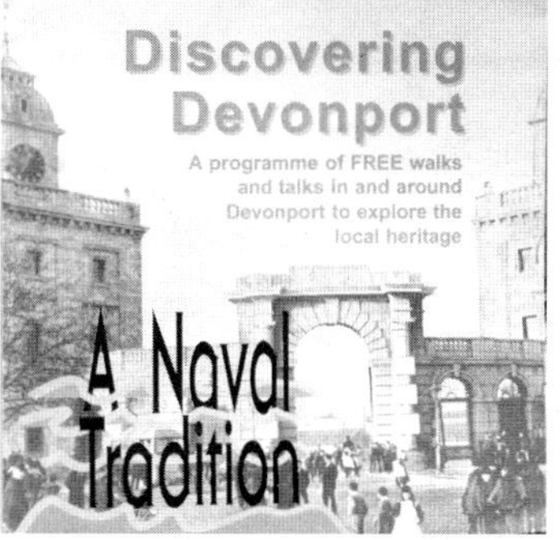

2002

Princess Anne officially opened the new Tamar Road Bridge extensions, the Duke of Edinburgh opened the new Vanguard Class submarine refit facility, and the first Trident submarine arrived at Devonport. The 6,000-ton cargo ship *Kadima* ran aground in Whitsand Bay and hundreds flocked to claim the timber booty. Various groups of local marines went off to fight the Taliban in Afghanistan. The Plymouth Mayflower, the city's latest tourist attraction, was opened on the site of Buddy's Diner, on the Barbican, overlooking the recently revamped Mayflower Memorial. For the second season in a row Albion won promotion, losing only three games, two of them to Orrell who pipped them on points difference in the last match of the season. Argyle finished champions of Division Three, setting a new record number of points for the division - 102 - and establishing various other club records along the way, among them French goalkeeper Romain Larrieu's 26 clean sheets. Estover College junk band Weapons Of Sound marked their tenth anniversary year with an invitation to play the Queen's Jubilee Concert at Buckingham Palace, and the smash hit musical *Chicago* was staged at the Theatre Royal, and *Buddy*, the show that had started life in Plymouth, made a successful return. Meanwhile tributes flooded in for colourful Barbican-based artist Robert Lenkiewicz, who died in August.

EVENING
Herald
Special Edition
24-page commemorative supplement of the Queen Mother's life inside today
THE QUEEN MOTHER
Born August 4, 1900. Died March 30, 2002
A NATION MOURNS

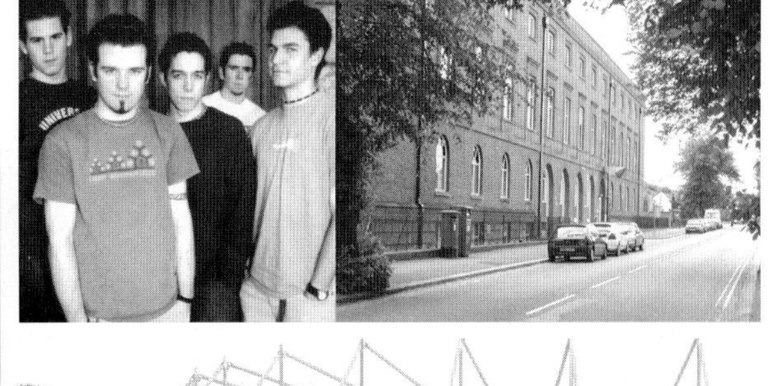

ACKNOWLEDGMENTS

Having taken hundreds of photographs of Plymouth over the last thirty years or so, I know how important it is to date and describe images as you take them; however, like most people who churn out such pictures, and who are invariably working to deadlines, I know too that most people leave that sort of thing "for another day". Consequently it has been hard to date some images precisely, hard to identify all the characters featured, and hard, in many cases, to identify the photographer responsible. Where possible I have endeavoured to credit the individuals concerned, having previously sought their permission to use the images in question. With almost 1,000 images in the book, most with no details accompanying them, this has not always been possible and as I also know how infuriating it is to find your work used without any credit whatsoever, may I therefore apologise now to anyone who feels neglected in this respect and may I add that the publishers would be happy to hear from anyone who has information concerning the copyright of any uncredited images. That said, a big thank you, in no particular order, is due to the following: Roy Westlake, city photographer who made his extensive archive of professional photographs of the Fifties, Sixties and beyond freely available; Mike Cox, *Herald* snapper throughout most of this Elizabethan period; Roy Todd, who took some excellent colour shots of Plymouth in the late Fifties and early Sixties; Dougie Flood, who similarly shot many fine scenes of Plymouth being rebuilt and in party mood around 1953. Robert Crane, who availed me of his father Harvey's wonderful collection of theatrical pictures, programmes and posters; Terry Guswell, who filled in the gaps in my season-by-season Argyle programme collection and provided essential technical support; Sylvia Boulden, for allowing me to rifle through her collection of images; Peter Waterhouse, for much the same; Mike Brown, for searching out pictures and information on Plymouth's darts celebrities; Jeanne Parrish and Mina Chapman, for availing me of their late husbands' Mayoral Year Books; Vernon Penprase, Jon Saberton, Hattie Hayne, Rob Warren, Jim Griffin, Dave Behennah, Daryle Gay, Crispin Gill, Edith Jury, John Waters, John Tozer, and a very large number of *Looking Back* readers. Thanks too, simply for taking great pictures, to Tony Carney, Al Stewart, Johnny Allen, Brian Jones, and the late Dermott Fitzgerald. Not forgetting Mark Tosdevin and Fiona Pitt at Plymouth City Museum & Art Gallery, Joyce Brown and the staff at Plymouth Local Studies Library, DML, Paul Kelly, Plymouth City Arts Officer, the Arts Centre, Plymouth Argyle FC, Bob Mills and all at Latimer Trend, and last but not least, Alan Qualtrough of the *Evening Herald* and Joan, Nicki and Nicky who look after the picture archive there.

On a practical note thanks to Doreen Mole for annotating and filing so much of my collection of personal and other photographs, images, programmes, posters and brochures, and to Ben Robinson whose first serious foray into the photographic world has been the digital capturing of the vast majority of these images. Thanks, too, to the rest of the family who allowed me to create more than 50 piles of pictures over a period of weeks and to clutter the Robinson establishment with boxes and boxes of "things that might come in useful for the book". Thanks to Clare, Des, Trish, Doreen, Michael Thrasher, Colin Rallings and a special eleventh hour thanks for the professional eyes of Jon Massey and Bill Bugler, without whose invaluable assistance ... And a big thank you to Douglas Fletcher and the Plymouth & South West Co-operative for their very welcome sponsorship of this project.

To Eric Dancer, Brigadier Miles Hunt-Davies and HRH The Duke of Edinburgh, and finally thanks to you for buying this book, thereby encouraging production of a 1900-1950 collection one of these days!

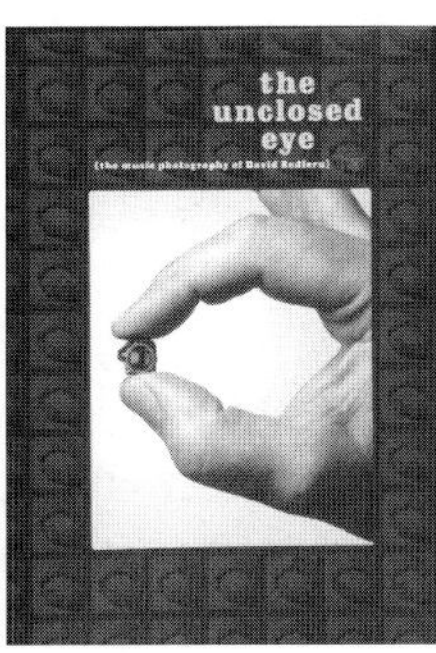

BIBLIOGRAPHY

All About Argyle, WS Tonkin, EJ Rickard (1963)
An A-Z of Everything, Trevor Montague, Little Brown & Company (2001)
Christmas Cheer, ed. Crispin Gill (1955-65)
Fire in Their Bones, Guy Fleming, Chapel Way (2002)
Fleet History of Plymouth Corporation and Plymouth City Bus Limited, PSV Circle (1994)
Making of Plymouth University, Alston Kennerley, University of Plymouth (2000)
125 Years with the Western Morning News, James Mildren, Bossiney (1985)
Plymouth A New History, Crispin Gill, Devon Books (1993)
Plymouth, A Portrait, JC Trewin, Robert Hale (1973)
Plymouth A Pictorial History, Guy Fleming, Phillimore (1995)
Plymouth Argyle - A Complete Record, Brian Knight, Breedon Sports Books (1989)
Plymouth As TIme Draws On, Vols I & II, Chris Robinson, Pen & Ink (1985, 1988)
Plymouth in Pictures, Crispin Gill, David & Charles (1968)
Plymouth: Maritime City in Transition, Chalkley, Dunkerley, Gripaios, David & Charles (1991)
Plymouth Steam 1954-63, Ian H Lane, Ian Allen (1984)
Plymouth The Waterfront City, Joy David, David (2002)
Plymouth Through the Lens, Nos 1-6, Brian Moseley, BS Moseley (1985-1993)
Pubs of Plymouth Past and Present, Vols I & II, Chris Robinson (1996, 1997)
Royal Visits to Devon and Cornwall, John Van Der Kiste, Halsgrove (2002)
Sutton Harbour, Crispin Gill, Devon Books (1997)
20th Century News, Lynne St Clair, Western Morning News (2000)
The Unclosed Eye, David Redfern, Sanctuary Music Library (1999)
Union Street, Chris Robinson, Pen & Ink (2000)
Vanishing Plymouth, Brian Moseley, BS Moseley (1982)

ELIZABETHAN PLYMOUTH – PICTURE INDEX

DUKE OF EDINBURGH: With Lord Mayor, George Wingett (*WMN*); At the NMA (*Mike Cox*)

CHRIS ROBINSON; My first wheels 1959; Navy Days 1966 (Chris Robinson): 44 New Street - first Barbican Studio 1979 *(Jon Sterk)*: Launch of first book at Theatre Royal with John Mills, Mayor and Mayoress 1985 (*Mike Cox*): With Alan Tibbitts of Video Ex and Mayor Tom Savery and wife Margaret at launch of millennium video Plymouth 2000 (*Clare Robinson*). With Keith Loze on Co-op Way (*Guy Channing*)

CO-OP; Co-op ad. 1953: Co-op 2002: Horse-drawn delivery van; Co-op van with roundsman Douglas Robertson (*Dermot Fitzgerald*): Co-op interior 1960s: Co-op building (*Roy Westlake*), Top floor: New Co-op shop in the Old Chapel, Devonport 2001.

QUEEN ELIZABETH II; Princess Elizabeth and Princess Margaret Rose on board HMS *Duke of York* at Devonport. 1947 (*WEH*): Princess Elizabeth laying stone at St Andrew's Church, 1949: Royal Silver Jubilee visit, 1977: Queen opening Manadon extension, 1983: Sundial "opening" 1988: Queen visits Royal William Yard 1992: Same visit 1992 (*WEH*).

1950: New Woolworths Building from Royal Parade (*WMN*): Little Dock Lane, Honicknowle and Tamar Way, Higher St Budeaux (Mike Parriss): Bush Radio Factory, Ernesettle (*Dermot P Fitzgerald*): Opening Woolworths (*WEH*): PC John Kelland with Trevor and Raymond Morrow (John Kelland): Mumfords 50th Anniversary (brochure pics): Michael Foot and Labour Party campaigners (*WEH*): Lucy Middleton canvassing (*WEH*): FA Cup holders Wolverhampton Wanderers visit Home Park (PAFC): Hill Lane Tennis Club players Anthony Aburrow, Barry George, Graham Morris, Val Sims, Leon Rosevere, Joan Smith, Rachel Cutler, Pat Lee with Mr Whiteford: Argyle Stars – William Shortt, Stanley Williams, Maurice Tadman, George Dews, William Strauss, Pat Jones and Neil Dougall (PAFC).

1951: Dingles completed (*Doug Flood*): Royal Parade; Pearl Assurance Building under construction; St Andrew's Cross; Armada Way looking north (*WEH*): Hill Lane tennis players with Angela Mortimer and Toni Cook (Toni Cook): Wilton Street; Gas Lighting (Mike Parriss): Planning the new Grandstand at Home Park (Jim Griffin): NAAFI postcard; Plympton Players with a young David Owen (John & Sylvia Boulden)

1952: Princess Margaret arrives in Plymouth to open new NAAFI; looking up North Hill; the new NAAFI; Princess Margaret outside NAAFI (*WMN*) Outing setting off from Corn Exchange (Shirley Walker): Young student radiographers (Gordon Tope): Bing Crosby arrives on liner in Plymouth (*Norman Hine*): Argyle celebration coaches; Argyle Champions (PAFC), Jumbo Chisholm (*WEH*).

1953: Coronation decorations; Odeon (Jeanette Simpson): Queen mother on visit to Royal Naval Barracks (*WMN*): Drake and Queen Elizabeth I figures in Royal Parade; Decorations; Sailors in Royal Parade (*Doug Flood*); Royal Parade approaches completion (*Roy Westlake*): Boots being built, Old Town Street: Dingles; Human chess on West Hoe, (*Doug Flood*): Royal Parade (Crispin Gill): Band On The Hoe at Hoe Pageant, Bowls match on The Hoe (*Doug Flood*): HMS *Salisbury* (*WEH*): Syncopating Sandy (Sylvia Boulden).

1954: Newly completed Pearl Assurance Building (*Doug Flood*): Temporary shops in Princess Square, and Cornwall Street (*Roy Westlake*): Cornwall Street (*Doug Floyd*): Plymouth Swing Club (Sheila Cook): Radiant House (*Roy Westlake*): Frederick Street, Keyham (Maureen Graham): Brian Hitchcock, speedway rider at Pennycross Stadium (John Walters): Sheila Pester and Brian Bishop of Ted Coleman's Band perform at Tecalemit Ball (Sheila Cook).

1955: City Centre under construction (*WMN*): Princess Square with temporary shops: New Boots Store (*Roy Westlake*): New George Street, two views (Sylvia Boulden): Michael Foot and Jennie Lee at Devonport Labour meeting; BBC Plymouth studio (*WMN*): Ted Colman's band at HMS *Drake* (Denise Putt): Staff at British Home Stores, opening day (Pauline Meatherell): Plymouth Motor Cycle Club (Sylvia Tatton): Moorfield School trip (Liz Rook): Embankment Garage (Mina Chapman).

1956: Queen Elizabeth the Queen Mother drives along the flight deck of HMS *Ark Royal* (*Doidge's Annual*): Derry's Clock and latest phase of Co-op development (*WMN*): HMS *Vanguard* and HMS *Unicorn* join the "mothball fleet" (*WMN*): Site of Drake Cinema, Union Street (City Museum): Co-op outing (Barbara Taylor): Circus coming down Alma Road (Crispin Gill): Compton Garage (Mina Chapman): Model boats (Gill): A1 skiffle group the Astor Institute Youth Club (Terry Horan): Telegram Boys (Palmer): Trelawny School netball team; football team (Ron Baldry).

1957: Crowd flock on to Hoe to see replica *Mayflower* in Sound (Local Studies Library): Post Office under construction (*Roy Westlake*): Replica of *Mayflower* in Sound (Local Studies Library): Spread Eagle, Treville Street (City Museum): The Steeljacks (Terry Horan): Kitto Centre (City Museum):Odeon and Barley Sheaf (*Doug Flood*): Barley Sheaf (City Museum): Joan Vickers MP, second right (WMN): Bottom of Cambridge Street (City Museum): Sailors in uniform (Doidges): HMS *Amethyst* being broken up at Marrowbone Slip (Crispin Gill): Blight & White Ad: Early stages of Bretonside (*Doug Flood*).

1958: Duke Of Edinburgh, with Lord Mayor George Wingett, visits Plymouth (*WMN*): Bretonside Bus Station completed: Duke of Edinburgh opens YMCA (Crispin Gill): Argyle v Newcastle at Home Park (*WEH*): Keppel's Head, Devonport (City Museum): Bretonside, two views (Sylvia Boulden): Kings Road Station (City Museum): Armada Way (*WMN*): Berkertex outing (Jean Johns):

1959: The Queen Mother with Percy Washbourne, Lord Mayor, visits newly re-constructed Guildhall (*WEH*): Newly completed St Andrew's Church (John Stevens): Opening day of the Pannier Market (*Roy Todd*): Royal Parade (Crispin Gill): Plympton Station; Glenholt Caravan Park (Sylvia Boulden): Inside the market (*Roy Westlake*): Brunel Bridge centenary lighting (Sylvia Boulden): Harry Moreton at St Andrew's organ (John Stevens): Argyle promotion team led out by Len Casey (PAFC): Penlee School (Edith Jury): North Road Station: (City Museum).

1960: York Street, now Western Approach; Guinness Clock, Drake Circus (*Roy Todd*): Co-op laundry staff Christmas party at Dolphin Rest (DM Bartrop): Tamar Bridge under way; North Road Station (*Roy Todd*): Union Street (City Museum): Old Town Street (*Roy Todd*): Co-op, North Quay; The George Tavern, Stonehouse (City Museum): Old Town Street and the Big Top, Central Park (*Roy Todd*): Public Central Rounders Team Joan Kelly, Sandra Wright, Sylvia Andrews, Veronica Hill, Janet Brook, front Beryl Bullard, Hazel Bartlett, Margaret Lamb, Janet Bettesworth and Valerie Carbines.

1961: Last Saltash Ferry (*Roy Todd*): Mayor of Saltash on last ferry (Peter Skinnard): Tamar Bridge under construction (*K Johnstone*): Plymouth Transport lorry (Peter Williamson): Opening of Laira Bridge, two views (*Roy Todd*): Hideaway Café (Daryle Gay): Westward TV under construction (*WMN*): Motorcyclists (Daryle Gay): Barbican (*Roy Westlake*):

1962: The Queen opens Civic Centre (*Roy Westlake*): Aerial view of city centre (*WMN*): Royal party outside Civic Centre (*Roy Westlake*): Civic Centre (Jim Griffin): Queen Mother, with Sir Clifford Tozer opening Tamar Bridge (*WMN*): New Council Chamber (Jim Griffin): Angela Collins (Harvey Crane): Behind the bar (LB): Turnbull's Garage (Jim Griffin): Darts Champion Fred Pritchard (Mike Brown): The Hepcats (LB): Barbican (*Roy Todd*): Argyle v Spurs (Peter Skinnard): Argyle v Spurs (PAFC).

1963: City Centre (*Roy Westlake*): St Andrew's Cross in the snow; Plymouth Zoo (*Roy Westlake*): Fourways Group (Terry Horan): Prince Rock Youth Club (*Mike Cox*): Gus Honeybun (Jim Griffin): ABC and Plaza (*WMN*): Dusty Springfield at the Majestic (Valerie Watts): Jon's, Mayflower Street (Jon Saberton): Stock cars with Roy Goodman (John Walters): BBC's Sheila Tracey (Gill): Westward Studio (Jim Griffin).

1964: Old Town Street (Fernley Wallis): New George Street (*Roy Westlake*): Harvest Home (LB): Eggbuckland (*WMN*): Mike Antonucci plus band (Mike Antonucci): Broad Park Road (*Pop Goddard*): Crazy golf on Hoe (*Roy Westlake*): Bobby C at the Majestic (Bobby C): Beatles at the ABC (*Mike Cox*): Keith Fordyce: Prince Regent Ballroom (*Roy Westlake*): Mr Garland and the Hyde Park Juniors, including Gregory Myatt, Chris Wood, Gerald Edmunds, Nigel Fisher, Ian Smith, Peter Colton, Andy Thomas and Mike Cook (Peter Colton).

1965: Mount Wise; Central Park Swimming Pool (*Roy Westlake*): Jill Robins star of HMS *Drake*'s *Jack and the Beanstalk* (Harvey Crane): Mike Turner, Majestic DJ (Mike Turner): Penlee School trip to Innsbruck, Gus Honeybun and Westward TV Studios (*WMN*): The Betterdays (Mike Hayne): Boots interior (*Roy Westlake*): Stock Cars, Johnny Marquand at Pennycross (Rob Warren): Frank Lord (PAFC): Folk singers Cyril Tawney and Lewis Johns (Lewis Johns): Ray Roach scores for Albion v Newton Abbot (*Mike Cox*).

1966: Art College Students (Hattie Hayne): Drake Circus (*WMN*): Target Boutique (Hattie Hayne): The old Tech College; HMS *Eagle* (*WEH*): Police 1100s, Guildhall Square (John Kelland): Mods on Scooters at St Andrews Cross (WEH): : Southside Street; Sabbath Day fight, Freedom Fields (*WMN*): Albion (*Mike Cox*):

1967: John, Paul, George and Ringo - The Beatles on The Hoe (*Dave Redfern*): Awaiting Chichester's return; Sir Francis Chichester with Lord Mayor Frank Chapman; Chichester sets foot on land; (Mina Chapman): Final parade of Plymouth Police (Dave Behennah): Cars in the parade (Len Hare) Southway; The Southway; Ernesettle (*WMN*): Stockcars at Pennycross Stadium (Rob Warren):

1968: Tecalemit Factory; exterior and interior; Duke of Edinburgh at Tecalemit (Mina Chapman): *Scylla* last warship build in Devonport, Miss Plymouth (*WMN*): Miss Keyham (Maureen Graham): *Scylla* team (Mary Wills): Rees Youth Centre, Plympton, Plympton general view (Mina Chapman): Plymstock School (*WMN*): Pirate Radio with Derek Jacobs (*John Tozer*): Milk float in Linketty Lane (*WMN*): TSB (Crispin Gill): Speedway, Pennycross, Fred Osborne, Phil Woodcock, Frank Payne, Den Jewell, Dave Whitaker, Keith Marks, Peter Lansdale Tony George with Mike Cake and Tony Leaves on bike (John Walters).

1969: Mr & Mrs Edmund Battle and dog Jim (*WMN*): City Centre; Site of Holiday Inn (*Roy Westlake*): West Hoe (LB): Stuart Huchinson (M Lloyd): The Oporto (*WMN*): Angela Rippon at her old school, Honicknowle (*WMN*): Mayflower Street (Roy Westlake) Reg Watts, Sandra Coe, Janet Brown, Paul Reeder, Richard Oliver at Carhullen Tennis Club (*WEH*): Speedway (John Walters).

1970: Duke of Edinburgh, with Deputy Lord Mayor, Walter Ainsworth in Southside Street (*WMN*); Jon Saberton's new store in Drake Circus (Jon Saberton): Art College with Monzo, fish seller (*Bill Shepherd*): Magnet Restaurant; Miss Plymouth; Caravan Park, Plym Woods; Pilgrims; Millbay Docks; Central Post Office; (*Roy Westlake*): Tim Green, darts (Mike Brown): Mayflower Bus (LSL): New shops at Southway; Last train from Millbay (*WMN*).

1971: Robert Lenkiewicz with mural (*WMN*): *Kathleen & May* (*Roy Westlake*): Kings Road Station; Crownhill (*WMN*): HMS *Albion* (David Coombs): Kings Road Station (*WMN*): Plymouth College Cyclists (Plymothian): Duke of Edinburgh with Mayor Dorothy Innes; new SWEB building; Rod Mason (*WMN*): Plymouth College 1st XI; Geoff Lawrence, David Bryant, Keith Johnson, John Martin, Nigel Baxter, Chris Wood, Ian Smith, Nick Bridge, front, Rob Hill, Kingsley Bishop, Roger Noble, Mike Penhall and K Newton (Plymothian).

1972: Armada Way (*Roy Westlake*): New Armada Way underpass, SWEB interiors, exterior (*WEH*): Leaving the Yard (Maurice Essery): OPOs annual dinner (LB): Plymouth Zoo (*Roy Westlake*): Ivy Benson Band (*WMN*): Bob Wilson, Jim Furnell at Bill Harper's Testimonial, Ray Bowden, Bob Wilson, Bill Harper, Jim Furnell and Peter Ballac (*Mike Cox*).

1973: Central Park paddling pool (Roy Westlake): New underpass; Ferry Kerisnel (*WMN*): Marsh Mills (Terry Guswell): Ford; Mutley Plain; Marsh Mills; Armada Way (*WMN*): Argyle (PAFC): Graham Little, Alf Ramsey at International, at Home Park (Graham Little): *Orpheus In The Underworld* (Harvey Crane).

1974: College of Further Education almost complete (Terry Guswell): Drake Circus (Jon Saberton): Bowls on The Hoe (Terry Guswell): Jon's interior (Jon Saberton): Royal Ballet big top in Central Park: Roy Lipscombe and Tony Waiters (*WEH*): Cliff "Ticker" Inglis, from the Longroom pub Stonehouse wins the first ever World Masters Darts Championship (Mike Brown): Hugh Scully presents Spotlight (*WEH*):

1975: North Road Station; Armada Way; College Of Further Education (Terry Guswell): Mike Westbrook and John Surman recording Citadel/Room 315 for RCA (*WMN*): Roy Slater, British rod-caught record sea bass (Chris Slater): Crown Matrimonial with Ian Stirling (Harvey Crane): Argyle, Paul Mariner and Billy Rafferty (*WEH*): *Candida*, with Matthew Arnold and Carole Bolland (Harvey Crane).

1976: St Andrew's Street (*WEH*): Brymon Airways (Terry Guswell): : Ian Stirling and Philip Madoc in *Sleuth*; Sid Livingstone and Geoffrey Saunders in Plymouth Theatre Company's *Gilbert & Sullivan* (Harvey Crane): Sharon Davies, 13, Plymstock School - youngest member of British Olympic swimming team: Plymstock Broadway, Fiesta Suite, DJ, Argyle (*WEH*).

1977: Silver Jubilee Royal Visit, Queen meets Big Chief, Michael Douglas; Princess Margaret visits Plymouth (*WMN*): David Owen, Foreign Secretary, opens Institute for Marine Environmental Research; Princess Anne visits Plymouth Tesco; Paul Mariner, Trevor Francis in Pilgrim shirts for Jim Furnell's testimonial (*WMN*): Plymouth College centenary collage (Plymothian): Jubilee Poster (*Chris Robinson*): Sheila Williams, Liz Hollister, Geoffrey Sloggett and Owen Morcom in the Tamaritan's production of Children's Day; David Meredith, Kate Lock, Gwenda Hughes in *Hobson's Choice*; Mark Rogers and David Davenport in the *Winslow Boy*; the cast of Aladdin at the Hoe Theatre (Harvey Crane): Sharon Davis and David Wilkie (*WMN*).

1978: *Ark Royal* returns; Prince Charles on board *Eye of the Wind*, Plymouth; *Ark Royal*: Argyle, with Gary Megson (*Mike Cox*): Monster Gut (Dave Behennah): Bill Pearce, Robert Daniel and Stafford Williams (*Mike Cox*): *An Ideal Husband* with Ian East and Plymouth Theatre Company at the Athenaeum (Harvey Crane): Argyle action (*WEH*): Mike Brown, Devon Darts Captain (Mike Brown).

1979: Mutley Plain and Mutley Methodist Church; Coxside, Mutley Plain (*WMN*): Nick Sims with the Catholics (Dave Behennah): West Hoe; Fred Binney (*WEH*): Vernon Penprase (Tony Penprase): *Bedroom Farce* with Hugh Paddick, Nyree Dawn Porter, Tim Brook-Taylor and Leslie Phillips (Harvey Crane).

1980: Bowyers Factory (*Chris Robinson*): Barbican; Mutley Plain (*WMN*): John Sims in action (*Mike Cox*): Carolyn Seaward, Miss UK (*Pete Holdgate*), Union Street; Sharon Davies and Olympic silver medal (*WMN*):

1981: Theatre Royal under construction (*Daryle Gay*): Hoe Café; Lenkiewicz paints flying ducks in water-based paint over mural 1st April (*WMN*): Devonport market; Crownhill shops (*WEH*); Tony Dennis (*Mike Cox*): Jubilee Hotel and Burton Boys (*Dave James*): Vernon Penprase sponsored by Squires (Tony Penprase): Mayflower Steps; Three Crowns (*Chris Robinson*).

1982: Off to the Falklands, HMS *Ardent*; Theatre Royal opened by Princess Margaret; Hoe Theatre closes (*WMN*): Still from film *Remembrance*, shot in Plymouth (Mainline Pictures): Ian Gillan and Colin Eddy (*Mike Cox*), St Boniface College awaiting demolition (*WEH*): Ian Calvert all-star charity team with George Best and Paul Mariner; Ian Botham at Home Park (*Mike Cox*): Gary Oldman on Torpoint Ferry in *Remembrance* (Mainline Pictures): Box Office Theatre Royal, Artist, landlady Beryl Cook outside the Dolphin; Plymouth historian Crispin Gill, collects his OBE (*WMN*).

1983: Queen visits Manadon (*WMN*): New Continental Hotel (*Chris Robinson*): Michael Foot; Power boat racing in the Sound (*Mike Cox*): Champagne for Alan Clark at the Duke of Cornwall (*WEH*): Opening of Broadway Sports Shop with Zaheer Abbas (*Mike Cox*): Launch of Radio Devon with Mike Gibbons and Reg Brookes (Radio Devon): The Argyle squad (PAFC).

1984: HMS *Scylla* back in Dockyard, Tamar Brewery, Devonport, Donald Sinden (*WMN*): John Benns: Betty & Crispin Gill with Mayor and Mayoress, Thelma and Derek Mitchell, at opening of Plymouth Art Club's 57th Spring Exhibition (*WMN*): Kevin Hodges almost equalizes at Villa Park, FA Cup semi-final (*Mike Cox*).

1985: Freedom Fields; Greenbank Hospital (*Bruce Seabrook*), RAF Mountbatten; Robert Lenkiewicz and new Barbican mural (*Tony Carney*), RAF Mountbatten, weather station (*John Chapman*): Plymouth Presents playwright Chris Savery (*Chris Robinson*): Hospital interior; John Ingham, Michael Heseltine and Simon Day at Royal William Yard (*WMN*): England cricketer Ellison weds local girl, with Paul Downton, Alan Lamb, Derek Underwood, Martin Moxom and Chris Cowdrey (*Mike Cox*): OPM hockey team (*Bruce Seabrook*).

1986: Ambulance drivers; Derriford Hospital; Bus queue, Royal Parade (*WMN*): David Bassett, Reg Brookes and David Milne, DG of the BBC at Radio Devon (Radio Devon): Snow on Royal Parade (*Tony Carney*): Radio Devon presenters Ian Phillips and Jill Dando: Monroes; Snow causes chaos (*WMN*): Snow in City Centre (*Chris Robinson*): Lucy McLoughlin (*Marc Hill*): Carol Butler (*Mike Cox*): China House (*Chris Robinson*): Argyle with Miss Plymouth Argyle (*Mike Cox*).

1987: Pedestrianisation of City Centre; Sainsbury's Homebase later Toys'R'Us (*Guy Newman*): New George Street (*WMN*): HMS *Brilliant* in refit at Devonport Dockyard (*Simon Burt*): Western Approach Car Park complete (*WMN*): Brymon Airways, Lord Mayor Tony Parrish (Jeanne Parrish): Postman Pat on The Hoe, David Owen (*WMN*) Brymon Air Stewardesses (Jeanne Parrish): OPM RFC (*Geoff Bowden*): Marine band leads Lord Mayor's Day Parade, Plymouth Lifeboat launched by Lady Mayoress Jeanne Parrish: OPMs v Plymouth Albion with Paul Ackford and Gary Lovell; Plymouth Hockey Club and Roger Shobrook (*Mike Cox*): Philanthropists CC - Steve Lindsay, Ernie Bolster, John Shaw, Chris Robinson, Chris Wood, Michael Thrasher, Chris Furnival, front Paul Jeffrey, Kingsley Bishop.

1988: Queen inspects new Sundial (*WEH*), Dingles fire (*Tony Carney*): Plymouth Dome opens (*John Allen*): Robert Lenkiewicz and Lord Mayor, Gordon Draper (*Lynn Johnson*): Margaret Thatcher at Derriford Hospital: Wayne Sleep and Marti Caine (*WMN*), David and Debbie Owen, Drake 400 celebrations (*Jack Collins*): New sundial; Millbay (*Mike Cox*): Vauxhall Street flooding (*Tony Carney*): HMS *Plymouth* (*Mike Cox*):

1989: Princess Diana visits HMS *Cornwall* (*Adam Eastland*): Dingles (*WMN*): Princess Anne visits HMS *Amazon*; Princess Alexandra visits Plymouth (*Mike Cox*): Tinside; Marsh Mills (*WMN*): Chay Blyth; New RAF Memorial; Plymouth Admirals (*Mike Cox*): Richard Deacon; Dingles; Tommy Tynan; QAB (*WEH*).

1990: Prince Charles visits sponsored runners to Sunderland (*Richard Taylor*): Princess Anne visits HMS *Raleigh*; Duchess of York visits Plymouth; Princess Anne at the Tall Ships, in Sutton Harbour (Al Linford): City Centre Christmas lights (*Mike Cox*): Storms ravage the city, roof coming off at Millbay Docks (*John Chapman*): Tony Carr and Dr Sheila Cassidy (*Mike Cox*): Milk Race on The Hoe (*Al Linford*): Farleys' Factory in Hartley closes: Farleys' receiver Malcolm London (*Tony Carney*): Burleigh School comes down (*Mike Cox*): Karrallon (Simon Rushton): Watershed (*Sam Smith*): Chris Walker (*Mike Cox*).

1991: Prince & Princess of Wales visit Devonport (*Tony Carney*): Plymouth Pavilions leisure pool; Plymouth Pavilions (*WMN*): Marsh Mills (*Adam Eastland*): Hoe Foreshore (*WMN*): The Retreat (*Sam Smith*): David Bassett (Radio Devon): Plymouth Poly (PLS): Dame Janet Fookes (*WMN*): Plymouth CC (*Richard Taylor*)

1992: Queen visits Royal William Yard (*Richard Taylor*): HMS *Trafalgar* (*WMN*): HRH Queen Elizabeth (*Mike Cox*): Michael Ball sings One Step Out Of Time as Britain's Eurovision entry (Polydor): Mount Batten (*Guy Channing*): Simon James, children's author and illustrator (*Richard Taylor*) Dockyard ship (*WMN*): Red Arrows on The Hoe; Millbay Docks (*WMN*): Music of the night (*Robert Howarth*): The Family Cat: Alan Cooper and staff of the WMN & WEH, meet Prince Philip; Nuclear Submarine at HMS *Defiance*; The Retreat at the Pavilions; Plymouth Hockey Club (*WMN*): North Quay (*Mike Cox*).

1993: New *Western Evening Herald* and *Morning News* building at Derriford; Old offices in New George Street; Prince Charles at Montpelier Junior School; Herald editorial staff, Mike Longhurst, Alan Cooper and Keith Scrivener at work in New George Street; Architectural Award for WEH building with architect Nicholas Grimshaw far right (*WEH*): Pete Goss looks out across the Hamoaze (*John Lyne*) Brittany Ferry at Millbay (*WMN*): Pro-Trident demo; Herald support for Trident; Albion captain and farmer, Graham Dawe; Joey The Lips; Crispin Gill with his *Plymouth A New History* (*WMN*).

1994: Royal William Yard; aerial (*WMN*): Tony Blair and David Jamieson at Devonport Dockyard protests (*Susannah Binney*): Christmas in the City Centre; Barbican potter John Pollex; Prince Charles at HMS Raleigh (*WMN*) Sainsbury's March Mills (*WMN*): Local band River (*Al Stewart*) Chris Boyd (*Wayne Perry*): Argyle goalkeeper Alan Nicholls; British Offshore Circuit Powerboat Race (*WMN*).

1995: Old Fish Market; New Fish Market (*Chris Robinson*): Hugh Grant and Emma Thompson (*Susannah*

Binney): Torpoint Ferry (*Chris Robinson*): Cast of *Sense and Sensibility* at Saltram House (*Susannah Binney*): Plymouth Admirals (*Richard Taylor*): Weapons of Sound (*WMN*): Armada Way tromp d'oeil (*Simon Burt*): Ronnie O'Sullivan watches Dennis Taylor during the British Open at Plymouth Pavilions (*Paul Slater*): Scott Dann (*Al Stewart*): Vince Lee at the Swan, Devonport (*WEH*): Cover of *Scene Magazine*, showing local musicians outside Cooperage (Scene):

1996: Plymouth Argyle supporters at Wembley; Play-off winners; Soundwaves; Music of the Night (*Mike Cox*): Merry-Go-Round in the City Centre (*Guy Channing*): Dawn French, Swan interior (*WMN*) Soundwaves (PCC): Clarks Shoe Factory (*WMN*): Charles and Jo Dance at Drake Odeon for the premiere of *Sense and Sensibility (Ian Jackson*): Vernon Penprase and Barry McGuigan at the opening of O'Neills (Tony Penprase): The Chaddlewood, Plympton; The Prawn on the Barbican (*Chris Robinson*): Lois Fletcher (*WMN*): Lockyer's Quay (*Chris Robinson*): Sainsbury's interior (*Ben Robinson*): Ronnie Mauge's Wembley winner (*Tony Carney*).

1997: Dartington Glass works (*Ian Jackson*): National Marine Aquarium under construction; Plymouth Fish Market (*Wayne Perry*): Storms lash The Hoe; Grundig Mountain Bike Race, Newnham Park (*John Allen*): Maggie Harris, Paul Cookney, Mehri Burton, Kate McDougal, Mike Turner and Dev Mohan with the new Ultrasonic Surgical Aspirator (*Guy Channing*): Plymouth Cricket Club (*Mike Cox*): Plymouth Raiders (*WEH*): HMS *Beaver* returns (*Guy Channing*): Devonport Field Gun Crew at launch of new poster by Brian Pollard with Bill Hodges (*Al Stewart*): Plymouth Soundwaves Festival (*WMN*): Andy Hicks losing to Nigel Bond (*Al Stewart*): Andy Hicks Benson & Hedges Snooker Championship winner (*John Allen*): Home Park (*Al Stewart*): Matt Bellamy of Muse at Soundwaves Festival; Katie Tokus of Sha Gov at Soundwaves (*WMN*):

1998: National Marine Aquarium (*John Lyne*): Mike Leece, Chief Executive of NMA at opening ceremony (*Brian Jones*): Aquarium (*Al Stewart*): Turnbulls Garage becomes car park (*Guy Channing*): 5ive headline Radio 1 Roadshow on The Hoe (*Al Stewart*): National Fireworks Competition (*John Allen*): Jaeger Factory closes (*Brian Jones*): Robert Lenkiewicz shows Terry Waite his exhibition at Museum (*Al Stewart*): Street Theatre on the Barbican (*Mike Cox*): Michael Sobey, Plymouth and E.C.Club (*John Allen*): Mick Heathcote celebrates with Chris Billy (*WEH*): Tamar Rally, Newnham Park (*John Allen*): Raiders crowd at the Pavilions (*WEH*): Slam Dunking Daniel Okonkwo (*Al Stewart*) Dennis Taylor at the Pavilions (*Mike Cox*) Paul Brooks lifts Shaun Stevens for Albion (*Brian Jones*) Roal Paulisen at Newnham (*Guy Channing*).

1999: Eclipse on The Hoe, Video-ex crew on Citadel wall (*John Allen*): Caprice and Jonathan Ross open Warner Village (*WEH*): Special eclipse sun glasses (*WMN*): City Centre, Amy, Harriet, Megan (*Chris Robinson*): Millennium Tea Dance (*Samantha Prichard*): Beating the retreat on The Hoe, Millennium Eve (*John Allen*): Old Town Street (*Chris Robinson*): Duke of Edinburgh visits the NMA, two views (*Mike Cox*): Ben Harvey and Jock McClung of Electra Bowls Club at Victoria Park with Richard Deacon's Moor sculpture behind (*Mike Cox*): Yachts by Phoenix Wharf; Yacht Haven, Mountbatten; North Quay; the Hogshead, Royal Parade (*Chris Robinson*): Chloe and Ben show Compton School Millennium project to Nolan Sister (*WEH*).

2000: Millennium celebrations on The Hoe; Millennium celebrations (*John Allen*): inset, Hoe revellers (*Lucy Blake*): Union Rooms (*Chris Robinson*): Tamar Bridge widening (*WMN*): Union Street Production poster: City Centre (*Chris Robinson*): Argyle action with Wayne O'Sullivan; and Paul McGregor (*WEH*) Ben Knight (WMN): Christian Sleep - Vicious Circle CD (*Teri Cox and Jon Massey*):

2001: Albion greeted as Champions v Penzance (*John Allen*): Aerial shot of Derry's Cross (*WMN*): The old Home Park (*Chris Robinson*): Sir Francis Drake Bowling Club (*WEH*): Argyle action with Ian Stonebridge (*WEH*): Argyle PA Box staff, Terry Guswell, Chris Robinson, Des Robinson, Brian Jones, Malcolm Townrow (*Dave Rowntree*): Plymouth University; Bus Station Loonies; Jack Cham's Lounge Bar, Ebrington St.; The Roundabout, Drake Circus; Walker-Wingsail outside New Marine Aquarium (*Chris Robinson*): The Jam Band, Clive Hooper, Keith Russell, Mick Taylor, Don Fox and Bev Day (Mick Taylor).

2002: New Argyle Stadium; Division Three Champions (*WEH*): The new Plymouth Mayflower attraction on the Barbican; Pennycomequick Sorting Office; Hornblower in New Street The Smart Car on show; Home Park (*Chris Robinson*): Argyle directors Peter Jones and Paul Stapleton (*WEH*) Romain Larrieu (*Ben Robinson*): Natalie Cornah interviews Graham Dawe: Kularoos (*Chris Robinson*) Argyle action (*WEH*).

LORD MAYORS OF PLYMOUTH

1939 – 44 Rt Hon The Viscount Astor
1944 – 45 Henry George Mason
1945 – 46 Rt Hon Isaac Foot
1946 – 47 W Harry Taylor
1947 – 48 Herbert Perry
1948 – 49 Herbert Perry
1949 – 50 Frank Leatherby
1950 – 51 Mrs Jacquetta Marshall
1951 – 52 Randolph H Baker
1952 – 53 Henry E Wright
1953 – 54 Sir James Clifford Tozer
1954 – 55 Edmund Perry
1955 – 56 Edwin Broad
1956 – 57 William James Oats
1957 – 58 Leslie Francis Paul
1958 – 59 George John Wingett
1959 – 60 Percival N Washbourn
1960 – 61 Frederick John Scott
1961 – 62 Arthur Goldberg
1962 – 63 Henry George Mason
1963 – 64 Henry Pillar Pattinson
1964 – 65 Thomas Harold Watkins
1965 – 66 Percival Dorton Pascho
1966 – 67 Thomas HL Stanbury
1967 – 68 Frank Chapman
1968 – 69 Ivor Clarence Lowe
1969 – 70 George Ernest Hillyer Creber
1970 – 71 Eric Donald Nuttall
1971 – 72 Mrs Dorothy FW Innes
1972 – 73 Jack Lester Luce
1973 – 74 John Clifford Porter
1974 – 75 George Ernest H Creber
1974 – 75 Frederick William Johnson
1975 – 76 William Ivor Thompson
1976 – 77 Arthur Raymond S Floyd
1977 – 78 Robert Ramsey Thornton
1978 – 79 William Evan Evans
1979 – 80 Graham Joseph Jinks
1980 – 81 Ronald George King
1981 – 82 Ralph Vernon Morrell
1982 – 83 Reginald Cyril James Scott
1983 – 84 Derek Mitchell
1984 – 85 Peter Whitfield
1985 – 86 John Leslie Mills
1986 – 87 William Henry C Glanville
1987 – 88 Anthony Harold Parrish
1988 – 89 Gordon Andrew Draper
1989 – 90 Dennis Harold Dicker
1990 – 91 John Finnigan, BEM
1991 – 92 Mrs Betty Easton, OBE
1992 – 93 Ronald Simmonds
1993 – 94 John Richards
1994 – 95 Walter Ainsworth
1995 – 96 Peter Wood
1996 – 97 Mrs Sylvia Bellamy
1997 – 98 Mrs Joan Stopporton
1998 – 99 Mrs Eileen Evans
1999 – 00 Tom Savery
2000 – 01 Dennis Camp
2001 – 02 David Viney
2002 – 03 Ian Gordon

MEMBERS OF PARLIAMENT FOR PLYMOUTH

General Elections

1945 Michael Foot, *Devonport* (Labour), Bert Medland, *Drake* (L) Lucy Middleton, *Sutton* (L)
1950 Michael Foot, *Devonport* (L), Mrs Lucy Middleton, *Sutton* (L)
1951 Michael Foot, *Devonport* (L), Hon Jacob Astor, *Sutton* (Conservative)
1955 Joan Vickers, *Devonport* (C), Hon Jacob Astor, *Sutton* (C)
1959 Joan Vickers, *Devonport* (C), Ian Fraser, *Sutton* (C)
1964 Joan Vickers, *Devonport* (C), Ian Fraser, *Sutton* (C)
1966 Dame Joan Vickers, *Devonport* (C), David Owen, *Sutton* (L)
1970 Dame Joan Vickers, *Devonport* (C), David Owen, *Sutton* (L)
1974 David Owen, *Devonport* (L), Hon. Alan Clark, *Sutton* (C), Janet Fookes, *Drake* (C)
1974 David Owen, *Devonport* (L), Hon. Alan Clark, *Sutton* (C), Janet Fookes, *Drake* (C)
1979 David Owen, *Devonport* (L), Hon. Alan Clark, *Sutton* (C), Janet Fookes, *Drake* (C)
1983 David Owen, *Devonport* (SDP), Hon. Alan Clark, *Sutton* (C), Janet Fookes, *Drake* (C)
1987 David Owen, *Devonport* (SDP), Hon. Alan Clark, *Sutton* (C), Janet Fookes, *Drake* (C)
1992 David Jamieson, *Devonport* (L), Gary Streeter, *Sutton* (C), Dame Janet Fookes, *Drake* (C)
1997 David Jamieson, *Devonport* (L), Linda Gilroy, *Drake* (C)
2000 David Jamieson, *Devonport* (L), Linda Gilroy, *Drake* (C)